Python Game Programming By Example

A pragmatic guide for developing your own games with Python

Alejandro Rodas de Paz

Joseph Howse

[PACKT] open source✻
PUBLISHING   community experience distilled

BIRMINGHAM - MUMBAI

Python Game Programming By Example

First published: September 2015

Production reference: 1230915

Published by Packt Publishing Ltd.
Livery Place
35 Livery Street
Birmingham B3 2PB, UK.

ISBN 978-1-78528-153-2

www.packtpub.com

Credits

Authors
Alejandro Rodas de Paz

Joseph Howse

Reviewers
Benjamin Johnson

Dennis O'Brien

Acquisition Editors
Owen Roberts

Sonali Vernekar

Content Development Editor
Dharmesh Parmar

Technical Editor
Ryan Kochery

Copy Editor
Vikrant Phadke

Project Coordinator
Harshal Ved

Proofreader
Safis Editing

Indexer
Rekha Nair

Graphics
Jason Monteiro

Production Coordinator
Manu Joseph

Cover Work
Manu Joseph

About the Authors

Alejandro Rodas de Paz is a computer engineer and game developer from Seville, Spain.

He came across Python back in 2009, while he was studying at the University of Seville. Alejandro developed several academic projects with Python, from web crawlers to artificial intelligence algorithms. In his spare time, he started building his own games in Python. He did a minor in game design at Hogeschool van Amsterdam, where he created a small 3D game engine based on the ideas he learned during this minor.

He has also developed some open source projects, such as a Python API for the Philips Hue personal lighting system. You can find these projects in his GitHub account at https://github.com/aleroddepaz.

Prior to this publication, Alejandro collaborated with Packt Publishing as a technical reviewer on the book *Tkinter GUI Application Development Hotshot*.

I would like to thank my parents, Feliciano and María Teresa, for their absolute trust and support. They have been an inspiration to me and an example of hard work.

I would also like to thank my girlfriend, Lucía, for her love and for putting up with me while I worked on this book.

Joseph Howse is a writer, software developer, and business owner from Halifax, Nova Scotia, Canada. Computer games and code are imbibed in his earliest memories, as he learned to read and type by playing text adventures with his older brother, Sam, and watching him write graphics demos in BASIC.

Joseph's other books include *OpenCV for Secret Agents*, *OpenCV Blueprints*, *Android Application Programming with OpenCV 3*, and *Learning OpenCV 3 Computer Vision with Python*. He works with his cats to make computer vision systems for humans, felines, and other users. Visit `http://nummist.com` to read about some of his latest projects done at Nummist Media Corporation Limited.

I dedicate my work to Sam, Jan, Bob, Bunny, and my cats, who have been my lifelong guides and companions.

I congratulate my coauthor for producing an excellent compendium of classic examples of game development. I am grateful for the opportunity to add my chapter on checkers (draughts) and computer vision.

I am also indebted to the many editors and technical reviewers who have contributed to planning, polishing, and marketing this book. I have come to expect an outstanding team when working with Packt Publishing, and once again, all of them have guided me with their experience and saved me from sundry errors and omissions. Please meet the technical reviewers by reading their biographies here.

Finally, I want to thank my readers and everybody in the open source community. We are united in our efforts to build and share all kinds of projects and knowledge, paving the way for books such as this to succeed.

About the Reviewers

Benjamin Johnson is an experienced Python programmer with a passion for game programming, software development, and web design. He is currently studying computer science at The University of Texas at Austin and plans to specialize in software engineering. His most popular Python projects include an adventure game engine and a particle simulator, both developed using Pygame. You can check out Benjamin's latest Pygame projects and articles on his website at www.learnpygame.com.

> I would like to thank Packt Publishing for giving me the opportunity to read and review this excellent book!

Dennis O'Brien is the director of data science at Game Show Network Games. He studied physics at the University of Chicago as an undergraduate and completed his graduate studies in computer science from the University of Illinois, Chicago. He was the principal software engineer at Electronic Arts, a senior software engineer at Leapfrog Enterprises, and a lead game developer at Jellyvision Games.

www.PacktPub.com

Support files, eBooks, discount offers, and more

For support files and downloads related to your book, please visit www.PacktPub.com.

Did you know that Packt offers eBook versions of every book published, with PDF and ePub files available? You can upgrade to the eBook version at www.PacktPub.com and as a print book customer, you are entitled to a discount on the eBook copy. Get in touch with us at service@packtpub.com for more details.

At www.PacktPub.com, you can also read a collection of free technical articles, sign up for a range of free newsletters and receive exclusive discounts and offers on Packt books and eBooks.

https://www2.packtpub.com/books/subscription/packtlib

Do you need instant solutions to your IT questions? PacktLib is Packt's online digital book library. Here, you can search, access, and read Packt's entire library of books.

Why subscribe?

- Fully searchable across every book published by Packt
- Copy and paste, print, and bookmark content
- On demand and accessible via a web browser

Free access for Packt account holders

If you have an account with Packt at www.PacktPub.com, you can use this to access PacktLib today and view 9 entirely free books. Simply use your login credentials for immediate access.

Table of Contents

Preface

Welcome to *Python Game Programming By Example*. As hobbyist programmers or professional developers, we may build a wide variety of applications, from large enterprise systems to web applications made with state-of-the-art frameworks. However, game development has always been an appealing topic, maybe simply for creating casual games and not just for high-budget AAA titles.

If you want to explore the different ways of developing games in Python, a language with clear and simple syntax, then this is the book for you. In each chapter, we will build a new game from scratch, using several popular libraries and utilities. By the end of this book, you will be able to quickly create your own 2D and 3D games, and have a handful of Python libraries in your tool belt to choose from.

What this book covers

Chapter 1, Hello, Pong!, details the required software, its installation, and the basic syntax of Python: data structures, control flow statements, object orientation, and so on. It also includes the first game of the book, the classic "Hello, world" game.

Chapter 2, Cocos Invaders, introduces the cocos2d game engine and explains how to build a game similar to *Space Invaders* to put this knowledge into practice. Here, you learn the basics of collisions, input handling, and scene setup.

Chapter 3, Building a Tower Defense Game, is where you learn to develop a full-fledged game with cocos2d. This game includes some interesting components, such as a HUD and a main menu.

Chapter 4, Steering Behaviors, covers seemingly intelligent movements for autonomous characters. You will be adding these strategies gradually, in different levels of a basic game built with particle systems.

Chapter 5, Pygame and 3D, presents the foundations of 3D and guides you through the basic structure of an OpenGL program.

Chapter 6, PyPlatformer, is where you develop a 3D platformer game with all the techniques learned in the previous chapter.

Chapter 7, Augmenting a Board Game with Computer Vision, introduces the topic of computer vision, which allows software to learn about the real world via a camera. In this chapter, you build a system to analyze a game of checkers (draughts) in real time as players move pieces on a physical board.

What you need for this book

The projects covered in this book assume that you have installed Python 3.4 on a computer with Windows, Mac OS X, or Linux. We also assume that you have included pip during the installation process, since it will be the package manager used to install the required third-party packages.

Who this book is for

If you have ever wanted to create casual games in Python and you wish to explore the various GUI technologies that this language offers, then this is the book for you. This title is intended for beginners in Python with little or no knowledge of game development, and it covers step by step how to build seven different games, from the well-known *Space Invaders* to a classical 3D platformer.

Conventions

In this book, you will find a number of text styles that distinguish between different kinds of information. Here are some examples of these styles and an explanation of their meaning.

Code words in text, database table names, folder names, filenames, file extensions, pathnames, dummy URLs, user input, and Twitter handles are shown as follows: "For instance, on Ubuntu, you need to install the python3-tk package."

A block of code is set as follows:

```
new_list = []
for elem in collection:
    if elem is not None:
        new_list.append(elem)
```

Any command-line input or output is written as follows:

```
$ python --version
Python 3.4.3
```

New terms and **important words** are shown in bold. Words that you see on the screen, for example, in menus or dialog boxes, appear in the text like this: "Make sure that you check the **Tcl/Tk** option to include the library."

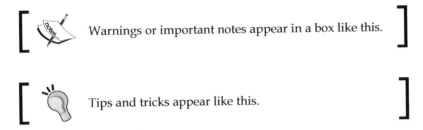

Warnings or important notes appear in a box like this.

Tips and tricks appear like this.

Reader feedback

Feedback from our readers is always welcome. Let us know what you think about this book—what you liked or disliked. Reader feedback is important for us as it helps us develop titles that you will really get the most out of.

To send us general feedback, simply e-mail feedback@packtpub.com, and mention the book's title in the subject of your message.

If there is a topic that you have expertise in and you are interested in either writing or contributing to a book, see our author guide at www.packtpub.com/authors.

Customer support

Now that you are the proud owner of a Packt book, we have a number of things to help you to get the most from your purchase.

Downloading the example code

You can download the example code files from your account at http://www.packtpub.com for all the Packt Publishing books you have purchased. If you purchased this book elsewhere, you can visit http://www.packtpub.com/support and register to have the files e-mailed directly to you.

Additionally, up-to-date example code for *Chapter 7, Augmenting a Board Game with Computer Vision*, is posted at http://nummist.com/opencv.

Downloading the color images of this book

We also provide you with a PDF file that has color images of the screenshots/diagrams used in this book. The color images will help you better understand the changes in the output. You can download this file from `https://www.packtpub.com/sites/default/files/downloads/B04505_Graphics.pdf`.

Errata

Although we have taken every care to ensure the accuracy of our content, mistakes do happen. If you find a mistake in one of our books—maybe a mistake in the text or the code—we would be grateful if you could report this to us. By doing so, you can save other readers from frustration and help us improve subsequent versions of this book. If you find any errata, please report them by visiting `http://www.packtpub.com/submit-errata`, selecting your book, clicking on the **Errata Submission Form** link, and entering the details of your errata. Once your errata are verified, your submission will be accepted and the errata will be uploaded to our website or added to any list of existing errata under the Errata section of that title.

To view the previously submitted errata, go to `https://www.packtpub.com/books/content/support` and enter the name of the book in the search field. The required information will appear under the **Errata** section.

Additionally, any errata for *Chapter 7, Augmenting a Board Game with Computer Vision*, will be posted at `http://nummist.com/opencv`.

Piracy

Piracy of copyrighted material on the Internet is an ongoing problem across all media. At Packt, we take the protection of our copyright and licenses very seriously. If you come across any illegal copies of our works in any form on the Internet, please provide us with the location address or website name immediately so that we can pursue a remedy.

Please contact us at `copyright@packtpub.com` with a link to the suspected pirated material.

We appreciate your help in protecting our authors and our ability to bring you valuable content.

Questions

If you have a problem with any aspect of this book, you can contact us at `questions@packtpub.com`, and we will do our best to address the problem.

You can also contact the authors directly. Alejandra Rodas de Paz, author of Chapters 1 to 6, can be reached at `alexrdp90@gmail.com`. Joseph Howse, author of Chapter 7, can be reached at `josephhowse@nummist.com`, and answers to common questions can be found on his website, `http://nummist.com/opencv`.

1
Hello, Pong!

Game development is a highly evolving software development process, and it has improved continuously since the appearance of the first video games in the 1950s. Nowadays, there are a wide variety of platforms and engines, and this process has been facilitated with the arrival of open source tools.

Python is a free high-level programming language with a design intended to write readable and concise programs. Thanks to its philosophy, we can create our own games from scratch with just a few lines of code. There are a plenty of game frameworks for Python, but for our first game, we will see how we can develop it without any third-party dependency.

In this chapter, we will cover the following topics:

- Installation of the required software
- An overview of **Tkinter**, a GUI library included in the Python standard library
- Applying object-oriented programming to encapsulate the logic of our game
- Basic collision and input detection
- Drawing game objects without external assets
- Developing a simplified version of *Breakout*, a pong-based game

Installing Python

You will need Python 3.4 with Tcl / Tk 8.6 installed on your computer. The latest branch of this version is Python 3.4.3, which can be downloaded from `https://www.python.org/downloads/`. Here, you can find the official binaries for the most popular platforms, such as Windows and Mac OS. During the installation process, make sure that you check the **Tcl/Tk** option to include the library.

The code examples included in the book have been tested against Windows 8 and Mac, but can be run on Linux without any modification. Note that some distributions may require you to install the appropriate package for Python 3. For instance, on Ubuntu, you need to install the `python3-tk` package.

Once you have Python installed, you can verify the version by opening Command Prompt or a terminal and executing these lines:

```
$ python --version
Python 3.4.3
```

After this check, you should be able to start a simple GUI program:

```
$ python
>>> from tkinter import Tk
>>> root = Tk()
>>> root.title('Hello, world!')
>>> root.mainloop()
```

These statements create a window, change its title, and run indefinitely until the window is closed. Do not close the new window that is displayed when the second statement is executed. Otherwise, it will raise an error because the application has been destroyed.

We will use this library in our first game, and the complete documentation of the module can be found at `https://docs.python.org/3/library/tkinter.html`.

Tkinter and Python 2

The Tkinter module was renamed to tkinter in Python 3. If you have Python 2 installed, simply change the `import` statement with `Tkinter` in uppercase, and the program should run as expected.

An overview of Breakout

The *Breakout* game starts with a paddle and a ball at the bottom of the screen and some rows of bricks at the top. The player must eliminate all the bricks by hitting them with the ball, which rebounds against the borders of the screen, the bricks, and the bottom paddle. As in *Pong*, the player controls the horizontal movement of the paddle.

The player starts the game with three lives, and if they miss the ball's rebound and it reaches the bottom border of the screen, one life is lost. The game is over when all the bricks are destroyed, or when the player loses all their lives.

This is a screenshot of the final version of our game:

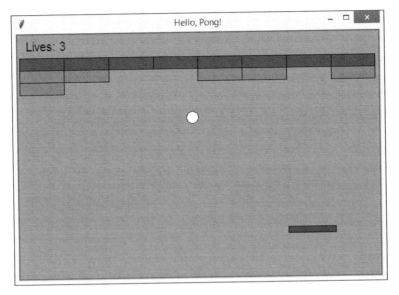

The basic GUI layout

We will start out game by creating a top-level window as in the simple program we ran previously. However, this time, we will use two nested widgets: a container frame and the canvas where the game objects will be drawn, as shown here:

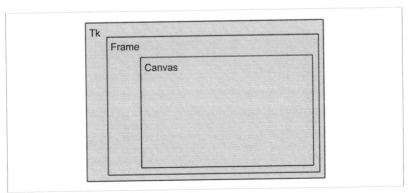

With Tkinter, this can easily be achieved using the following code:

```python
import tkinter as tk

lives = 3
root = tk.Tk()
frame = tk.Frame(root)
canvas = tk.Canvas(frame, width=600, height=400, bg='#aaaaff')
frame.pack()
canvas.pack()
root.title('Hello, Pong!')
root.mainloop()
```

Downloading the example code

You can download the example code files from your account at
http://www.packtpub.com for all the Packt Publishing books
you have purchased. If you purchased this book elsewhere, you can
visit http://www.packtpub.com/support and register to have
the files e-mailed directly to you.

Through the `tk` alias, we access the classes defined in the `tkinter` module, such as
`Tk`, `Frame`, and `Canvas`.

Notice the first argument of each constructor call which indicates the widget (the
child container), and the required `pack()` calls for displaying the widgets on their
parent container. This is not necessary for the `Tk` instance, since it is the root window.

However, this approach is not exactly object-oriented, since we use global variables
and do not define any new classes to represent our new data structures. If the code
base grows, this can lead to poorly organized projects and highly coupled code.

We can start encapsulating the pieces of our game in this way:

```python
import tkinter as tk

class Game(tk.Frame):
    def __init__(self, master):
        super(Game, self).__init__(master)
        self.lives = 3
        self.width = 610
        self.height = 400
        self.canvas = tk.Canvas(self, bg='#aaaaff',
                                width=self.width,
                                height=self.height)
```

```
        self.canvas.pack()
        self.pack()

if __name__ == '__main__':
    root = tk.Tk()
    root.title('Hello, Pong!')
    game = Game(root)
    game.mainloop()
```

Our new type, called `Game`, inherits from the `Frame` Tkinter class. The `class Game(tk.Frame):` definition specifies the name of the class and the superclass between parentheses.

If you are new to object-oriented programming with Python, this syntax may not sound familiar. In our first look at classes, the most important concepts are the `__init__` method and the `self` variable:

- The `__init__` method is a special method that is invoked when a new class instance is created. Here, we set the object attributes, such as the width, the height, and the canvas widget. We also call the parent class initialization with the `super(Game, self).__init__(master)` statement, so the initial state of the `Frame` is properly initialized.

- The `self` variable refers to the object, and it should be the first argument of a method if you want to access the object instance. It is not strictly a language keyword, but the Python convention is to call it `self` so that other Python programmers won't be confused about the meaning of the variable.

In the preceding snippet, we introduced the `if __name__ == '__main__'` condition, which is present in many Python scripts. This snippet checks the name of the current module that is being executed, and will prevent starting the main loop where this module was being imported from another script. This block is placed at the end of the script, since it requires that the `Game` class be defined.

New- and old-style classes

You may see the `MySuperClass.__init__(self, arguments)` syntax in some Python 2 examples, instead of the `super` call. This is the old-style syntax, the only flavor available up to Python 2.1, and is maintained in Python 2 for backward compatibility.

The `super(MyClass, self).__init__(arguments)` is the new-class style introduced in Python 2.2. It is the preferred approach, and we will use it throughout this book.

See the `chapter1_01.py` script, which contains this code. Since no external assets are needed, you can place it in any directory and execute it from the Python command line by running `chapter1_01.py`. The main loop will run indefinitely until you click on the close button of the window, or you kill the process from the command line.

This is the starting point of our game, so let's start diving into the Canvas widget and see how we can draw and animate items in it.

Diving into the Canvas widget

So far, we have the window set up and now we can start drawing items on the canvas. The Canvas widget is two-dimensional and uses the Cartesian coordinate system. The origin—the (0, 0) ordered pair—is placed in the top-left corner, and the axis can be represented as shown in the following screenshot:

Keeping this layout in mind, we can use two methods of the Canvas widget to draw the paddle, the bricks, and the ball:

- `canvas.create_rectangle(x0, y0, x1, y1, **options)`
- `canvas.create_oval(x0, y0, x1, y1, **options)`

Each of these calls returns an integer, which identifies the item handle. This reference will be used later to manipulate the position of the item and its options. The `**options` syntax represents a key/value pair of additional arguments that can be passed to the method call. In our case, we will use the `fill` and the `tags` option.

The x0 and y0 coordinates indicate the top-left corner of the previous screenshot, and x1 and y1 are indicated in the bottom-right corner.

For instance, we can call `canvas.create_rectangle(250, 300, 330, 320, fill='blue', tags='paddle')` to create a player's paddle, where:

- The top-left corner is at the coordinates *(250, 300)*.
- The bottom-right corner is at the coordinates *(300, 320)*.
- The `fill='blue'` means that the background color of the item is blue.
- The `tags='paddle'` means that the item is tagged as a paddle. This string will be useful later to find items in the canvas with specific tags.

We will invoke other Canvas methods to manipulate the items and retrieve widget information. This table gives the references to the Canvas widget that will be used in this chapter:

Method	Description
`canvas.coords(item)`	Returns the coordinates of the bounding box of an item.
`canvas.move(item, x, y)`	Moves an item by a horizontal and a vertical offset.
`canvas.delete(item)`	Deletes an item from the canvas.
`canvas.winfo_width()`	Retrieves the canvas width.
`canvas.itemconfig(item, **options)`	Changes the options of an item, such as the fill color or its tags.
`canvas.bind(event, callback)`	Binds an input event with the execution of a function. The callback handler receives one parameter of the type Tkinter event.
`canvas.unbind(event)`	Unbinds the input event so that there is no callback function executed when the event occurs.
`canvas.create_text (*position, **opts)`	Draws text on the canvas. The `position` and the `options` arguments are similar to the ones passed in `canvas.create_rectangle` and `canvas.create_oval`.
`canvas.find_withtag(tag)`	Returns the items with a specific tag.
`canvas.find_overlapping (*position)`	Returns the items that overlap or are completely enclosed by a given rectangle.

You can check out a complete reference of the event syntax as well as some practical examples at http://effbot.org/tkinterbook/tkinter-events-and-bindings.htm#events.

Basic game objects

Before we start drawing all our game items, let's define a base class with the functionality that they will have in common—storing a reference to the canvas and its underlying canvas item, getting information about its position, and deleting the item from the canvas:

```python
class GameObject(object):
    def __init__(self, canvas, item):
        self.canvas = canvas
        self.item = item

    def get_position(self):
        return self.canvas.coords(self.item)

    def move(self, x, y):
        self.canvas.move(self.item, x, y)

    def delete(self):
        self.canvas.delete(self.item)
```

Assuming that we have created a Canvas widget as shown in our previous code samples, a basic usage of this class and its attributes would be like this:

```python
item = canvas.create_rectangle(10,10,100,80, fill='green')
game_object = GameObject(canvas,item) #create new instance

print(game_object.get_position())
# [10, 10, 100, 80]
game_object.move(20, -10)
print(game_object.get_position())
# [30, 0, 120, 70]
game_object.delete()
```

In this example, we created a green rectangle and a GameObject instance with the resulting item. Then we retrieved the position of the item within the canvas, moved it, and calculated the position again. Finally, we deleted the underlying item.

The methods that the GameObject class offers will be reused in the subclasses that we will see later, so this abstraction avoids unnecessary code duplication. Now that you have learned how to work with this basic class, we can define separate child classes for the ball, the paddle, and the bricks.

The Ball class

The Ball class will store information about the speed, direction, and radius of the ball. We will simplify the ball's movement, since the direction vector will always be one of the following:

- **[1, 1]** if the ball is moving towards the bottom-right corner
- **[-1, -1]** if the ball is moving towards the top-left corner
- **[1, -1]** if the ball is moving towards the top-right corner
- **[-1, 1]** if the ball is moving towards the bottom-left corner

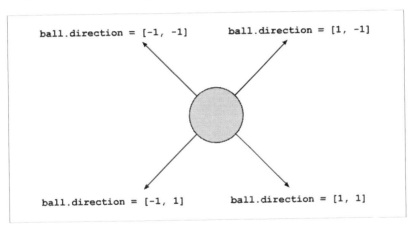

A representation of the possible direction vectors

Therefore, by changing the sign of one of the vector components, we will change the ball's direction by 90 degrees. This will happen when the ball bounces against the canvas border, when it hits a brick, or the player's paddle:

```
class Ball(GameObject):
    def __init__(self, canvas, x, y):
        self.radius = 10
        self.direction = [1, -1]
        self.speed = 10
        item = canvas.create_oval(x-self.radius, y-self.radius,
                                  x+self.radius, y+self.radius,
                                  fill='white')
        super(Ball, self).__init__(canvas, item)
```

For now, the object initialization is enough to understand the attributes that the class has. We will cover the ball rebound logic later, when the other game objects have been defined and placed in the game canvas.

The Paddle class

The `Paddle` class represents the player's paddle and has two attributes to store the width and height of the paddle. A `set_ball` method will be used to store a reference to the ball, which can be moved with the ball before the game starts:

```
class Paddle(GameObject):
    def __init__(self, canvas, x, y):
        self.width = 80
        self.height = 10
        self.ball = None
        item = canvas.create_rectangle(x - self.width / 2,
                                       y - self.height / 2,
                                       x + self.width / 2,
                                       y + self.height / 2,
                                       fill='blue')
        super(Paddle, self).__init__(canvas, item)

    def set_ball(self, ball):
        self.ball = ball

    def move(self, offset):
        coords = self.get_position()
        width = self.canvas.winfo_width()
        if coords[0] + offset >= 0 and \
            coords[2] + offset <= width:
            super(Paddle, self).move(offset, 0)
            if self.ball is not None:
                self.ball.move(offset, 0)
```

The `move` method is responsible for the horizontal movement of the paddle. Step by step, the following is the logic behind this method:

- The `self.get_position()` calculates the current coordinates of the paddle
- The `self.canvas.winfo_width()` retrieves the canvas width

- If both the minimum and maximum x-axis coordinates, plus the offset produced by the movement, are inside the boundaries of the canvas, this is what happens:
    - The super(Paddle, self).move(offset, 0) calls the method with same name in the Paddle class's parent class, which moves the underlying canvas item
    - If the paddle still has a reference to the ball (this happens when the game has not been started), the ball is moved as well

This method will be bound to the input keys so that the player can use them to control the paddle's movement. We will see later how we can use Tkinter to process the input key events. For now, let's move on to the implementation of the last one of our game's components.

The Brick class

Each brick in our game will be an instance of the Brick class. This class contains the logic that is executed when the bricks are hit and destroyed:

```python
class Brick(GameObject):
    COLORS = {1: '#999999', 2: '#555555', 3: '#222222'}

    def __init__(self, canvas, x, y, hits):
        self.width = 75
        self.height = 20
        self.hits = hits
        color = Brick.COLORS[hits]
        item = canvas.create_rectangle(x - self.width / 2,
                                       y - self.height / 2,
                                       x + self.width / 2,
                                       y + self.height / 2,
                                       fill=color,
                                       tags='brick')
        super(Brick, self).__init__(canvas, item)

    def hit(self):
        self.hits -= 1
        if self.hits == 0:
            self.delete()
        else:
            self.canvas.itemconfig(self.item,
                                   fill=Brick.COLORS[self.hits])
```

As you may have noticed, the `__init__` method is very similar to the one in the `Paddle` class, since it draws a rectangle and stores the width and the height of the shape. In this case, the value of the `tags` option passed as a keyword argument is `'brick'`. With this tag, we can check whether the game is over when the number of remaining items with this tag is zero.

Another difference from the `Paddle` class is the `hit` method and the attributes it uses. The class variable called COLORS is a dictionary—a data structure that contains key/value pairs with the number of hits that the brick has left, and the corresponding color. When a brick is hit, the method execution occurs as follows:

- The number of hits of the brick instance is decreased by 1
- If the number of hits remaining is 0, `self.delete()` deletes the brick from the canvas
- Otherwise, `self.canvas.itemconfig()` changes the color of the brick

For instance, if we call this method for a brick with two hits left, we will decrease the counter by 1 and the new color will be `#999999`, which is the value of `Brick.COLORS[1]`. If the same brick is hit again, the number of remaining hits will become zero and the item will be deleted.

Adding the Breakout items

Now that the organization of our items is separated into these top-level classes, we can extend the `__init__` method of our Game class:

```
class Game(tk.Frame):
    def __init__(self, master):
        super(Game, self).__init__(master)
        self.lives = 3
        self.width = 610
        self.height = 400
        self.canvas = tk.Canvas(self, bg='#aaaaff',
                                width=self.width,
                                height=self.height)
        self.canvas.pack()
        self.pack()

        self.items = {}
        self.ball = None
        self.paddle = Paddle(self.canvas, self.width/2, 326)
        self.items[self.paddle.item] = self.paddle
        for x in range(5, self.width - 5, 75):
```

```
            self.add_brick(x + 37.5, 50, 2)
            self.add_brick(x + 37.5, 70, 1)
            self.add_brick(x + 37.5, 90, 1)

        self.hud = None
        self.setup_game()
        self.canvas.focus_set()
        self.canvas.bind('<Left>',
                        lambda _: self.paddle.move(-10))
        self.canvas.bind('<Right>',
                        lambda _: self.paddle.move(10))

    def setup_game(self):
        self.add_ball()
        self.update_lives_text()
        self.text = self.draw_text(300, 200,
        'Press Space to start')
        self.canvas.bind('<space>',
        lambda _: self.start_game())
```

This initialization is more complex that what we had at the beginning of the chapter. We can divide it into two sections:

- **Game object instantiation**, and their insertion into the `self.items` dictionary. This attribute contains all the canvas items that can collide with the ball, so we add only the bricks and the player's paddle to it. The keys are the references to the canvas items, and the values are the corresponding game objects. We will use this attribute later in the collision check, when we will have the colliding items and will need to fetch the `game` object.

- **Key input binding**, via the Canvas widget. The `canvas.focus_set()` call sets the focus on the canvas, so the input events are directly bound to this widget. Then we bind the left and right keys to the paddle's `move()` method and the spacebar to trigger the game start. Thanks to the `lambda` construct, we can define anonymous functions as event handlers. Since the callback argument of the `bind` method is a function that receives a Tkinter event as an argument, we define a lambda that ignores the first parameter — `lambda _: <expression>`.

Our new `add_ball` and `add_brick` methods are used to create game objects and perform a basic initialization. While the first one creates a new ball on top of the player's paddle, the second one is a shorthand way of adding a `Brick` instance:

```
    def add_ball(self):
        if self.ball is not None:
            self.ball.delete()
```

```
        paddle_coords = self.paddle.get_position()
        x = (paddle_coords[0] + paddle_coords[2]) * 0.5
        self.ball = Ball(self.canvas, x, 310)
        self.paddle.set_ball(self.ball)

    def add_brick(self, x, y, hits):
        brick = Brick(self.canvas, x, y, hits)
        self.items[brick.item] = brick
```

The draw_text method will be used to display text messages in the canvas. The underlying item created with canvas.create_text() is returned, and it can be used to modify the information:

```
    def draw_text(self, x, y, text, size='40'):
        font = ('Helvetica', size)
        return self.canvas.create_text(x, y, text=text,
                                                font=font)
```

The update_lives_text method displays the number of lives left and changes its text if the message is already displayed. It is called when the game is initialized — this is when the text is drawn for the first time — and it is also invoked when the player misses a ball rebound:

```
    def update_lives_text(self):
        text = 'Lives: %s' % self.lives
        if self.hud is None:
            self.hud = self.draw_text(50, 20, text, 15)
        else:
            self.canvas.itemconfig(self.hud, text=text)
```

We leave start_game unimplemented for now, since it triggers the game loop, and this logic will be added in the next section. Since Python requires a code block for each method, we use the pass statement. This does not execute any operation, and it can be used as a placeholder when a statement is required syntactically:

```
    def start_game(self):
        pass
```

See the `chapter1_02.py` module, a script with the sample code we have so far. If you execute this script, it will display a Tkinter window like the one shown in the following figure. At this point, we can move the paddle horizontally, so we are ready to start the game and hit some bricks:

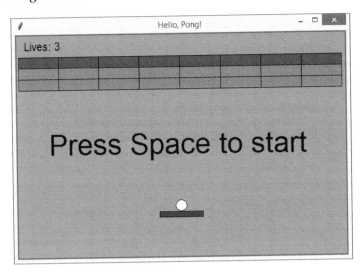

Movement and collisions

Now that we have placed all of our game objects, we can define the methods that will be executed in the game loop. This loop runs indefinitely until the game ends, and each iteration updates the position of the ball and checks the collision that occurs.

With the Canvas widget, we can calculate what the items that overlap with the given coordinates are, so for now, we will implement the methods that are responsible for moving the ball and changing its direction.

Let's start with the movement of the ball and the conditions for recreating the bouncing effect when it reaches the canvas borders:

```
def update(self):
    coords = self.get_position()
    width = self.canvas.winfo_width()
    if coords[0] <= 0 or coords[2] >= width:
        self.direction[0] *= -1
    if coords[1] <= 0:
        self.direction[1] *= -1
    x = self.direction[0] * self.speed
    y = self.direction[1] * self.speed
    self.move(x, y)
```

The **update** method does the following:

- It gets the current position and the width of the canvas. It stores the values in the `coords` and `width` local variables, respectively.
- If the position collides with the left or right border of the canvas, the horizontal component of the direction vector changes its sign
- If the position collides with the upper border of the canvas, the vertical component of the direction vector changes its sign
- We scale the direction vector by the ball's speed
- The `self.move(x, y)` moves the ball

For instance, if the ball hits the left border, the `coords[0] <= 0` condition evaluates to true, so the x-axis component of the direction changes its sign, as shown in this diagram:

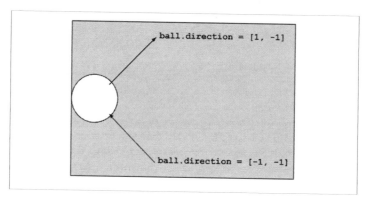

If the ball hits the top-right corner, both `coords[2] >= width` and `coords[1] <= 0` evaluate to true. This changes the sign of both the components of the direction vector, like this:

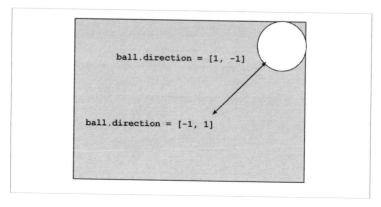

The logic of the collision with a brick is a bit more complex, since the direction of the rebound depends on the side where the collision occurs.

We will calculate the x-axis component of the ball's center and check whether it is between the lowermost and uppermost x-axis coordinates of the colliding brick. To translate this into a quick implementation, the following snippet shows the possible changes in the direction vector as per the ball and brick coordinates:

```
coords = self.get_position()
x = (coords[0] + coords[2]) * 0.5
brick_coords = brick.get_position()
if x > brick_coords[2]:
    self.direction[0] = 1
elif x < brick_coords[0]:
    self.direction[0] = -1
else:
    self.direction[1] *= -1
```

For instance, this collision causes a horizontal rebound, since the brick is being hit from above, as shown here:

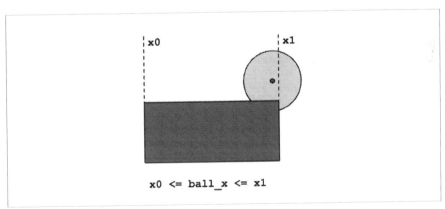

On the other hand, a collision from the right-hand side of the brick would be as follows:

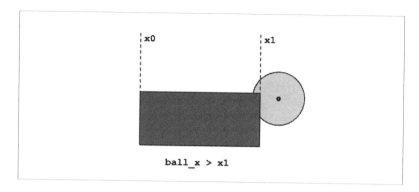

This is valid when the ball hits the paddle or a single brick. However, the ball can hit two bricks at the same time. In this situation, we cannot execute the previous statements for each brick; if the y-axis direction is multiplied by -1 twice, the value in the next iteration of the game loop will be the same.

We could check whether the collision occurred from above or behind, but the problem with multiple bricks is that the ball may overlap the lateral of one of the bricks and, therefore, change the x-axis direction as well. This happens because of the ball's speed and the rate at which its position is updated.

We will simplify this by assuming that a collision with multiple bricks at the same time occurs only from above or below. That means that it changes the y-axis component of the direction without calculating the position of the colliding bricks:

```python
if len(game_objects) > 1:
    self.direction[1] *= -1
```

With these two conditions, we can define the `collide` method. As we will see later, another method will be responsible for determining the list of colliding bricks, so this method only handles the outcome of a collision with one or more bricks:

```python
def collide(self, game_objects):
    coords = self.get_position()
    x = (coords[0] + coords[2]) * 0.5
    if len(game_objects) > 1:
        self.direction[1] *= -1
    elif len(game_objects) == 1:
        game_object = game_objects[0]
        coords = game_object.get_position()
        if x > coords[2]:
```

```
            self.direction[0] = 1
        elif x < coords[0]:
            self.direction[0] = -1
        else:
            self.direction[1] *= -1

    for game_object in game_objects:
        if isinstance(game_object, Brick):
            game_object.hit()
```

Note that this method hits every brick instance that is colliding with the ball, so the hit counters are decreased and the bricks are removed if they reach zero hits.

Starting the game

Finally, we have built the functionality needed to run the game loop—the logic required to update the ball's position according to the rebounds, and restart the game if the player loses one life.

Now we can add the following methods to our Game class to complete the development of our game:

```
def start_game(self):
    self.canvas.unbind('<space>')
    self.canvas.delete(self.text)
    self.paddle.ball = None
    self.game_loop()

def game_loop(self):
    self.check_collisions()
    num_bricks = len(self.canvas.find_withtag('brick'))
    if num_bricks == 0:
        self.ball.speed = None
        self.draw_text(300, 200, 'You win!')
    elif self.ball.get_position()[3] >= self.height:
        self.ball.speed = None
        self.lives -= 1
        if self.lives < 0:
            self.draw_text(300, 200, 'Game Over')
        else:
            self.after(1000, self.setup_game)
    else:
        self.ball.update()
        self.after(50, self.game_loop)
```

The `start_game` method, which we left unimplemented in a previous section, is responsible for unbinding the *Spacebar* input key so that the player cannot start the game twice, detaching the ball from the paddle, and starting the game loop.

Step by step, the `game_loop` method does the following:

- It calls `self.check_collisions()` to process the ball's collisions. We will see its implementation in the next code snippet.

- If the number of bricks left is zero, it means that the player has won, and a congratulations text is displayed.

- Suppose the ball has reached the bottom of the canvas:

    ○ Then, the player loses one life. If the number of lives left is zero, it means that the player has lost, and the **Game Over** text is shown. Otherwise, the game is reset

- Otherwise, this is what happens:

    ○ The position of the ball is updated according to its speed and direction, and the game loop is called again. The `.after(delay, callback)` method on a Tkinter widget sets a timeout to invoke a function after a delay in milliseconds. Since this statement will be executed when the game is not over yet, this creates the loop necessary to execute this logic continuously:

```
def check_collisions(self):
    ball_coords = self.ball.get_position()
    items = self.canvas.find_overlapping(*ball_coords)
    objects = [self.items[x] for x in items \
            if x in self.items]
    self.ball.collide(objects)
```

The `check_collisions` method links the game loop with the ball collision method. Since `Ball.collide` receives a list of game objects and `canvas.find_overlapping` returns a list of colliding items with a given position, we use the dictionary of items to transform each canvas item into its corresponding game object.

Remember that the `items` attribute of the `Game` class contains only those canvas items that can collide with the ball. Therefore, we need to pass only the items contained in this dictionary. Once we have filtered the canvas items that cannot collide with the ball, such as the text displayed in the top-left corner, we retrieve each game object by its key.

With list comprehensions, we can create the required list in one simple statement:

```
objects = [self.items[x] for x in items if x in self.items]
```

The basic syntax of list comprehensions is the following:

```
new_list = [expr(elem) for elem in collection]
```

This means that the `new_list` variable will be a list whose elements are the result of applying the `expr` function to each `elem` in the list collection.

We can filter the elements to which the expression will be applied by adding an `if` clause:

```
new_list = [expr(elem) for elem in collection if elem is not None]
```

This syntax is equivalent to the following loop:

```
new_list = []
for elem in collection:
    if elem is not None:
        new_list.append(elem)
```

In our case, the initial list is the list of colliding items, the `if` clause filters the items that are not contained in the dictionary, and the expression applied to each element retrieves the game object associated with the canvas item. The `collide` method is called with this list as a parameter, and the logic for the game loop is completed.

Playing Breakout

Open the `chapter1_complete.py` script to see the final version of the game, and run it by executing `chapter1_complete.py`, as you did with the previous code samples.

When you press the spacebar, the game starts and the player controls the paddle with the right and left arrow keys. Each time the player misses the ball, the lives counter will decrease, and the game will be over if the ball rebound is missed again and there are no lives left:

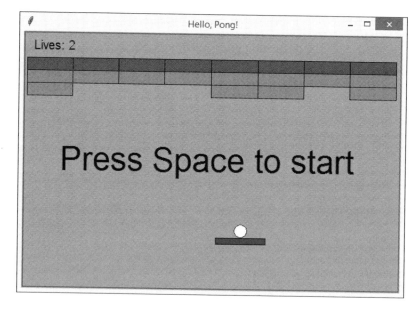

In our first game, all the classes have been defined in a single script. However, as the number of lines of code increases, it becomes necessary to define separate scripts for each part. In the next chapters, we will see how it is possible to organize our code by modules.

Summary

In this chapter, we built out first game with vanilla Python. We covered the basics of the control flow and the class syntax. We used Tkinter widgets, especially the Canvas widget and its methods, to achieve the functionality needed to develop a game based on collisions and simple input detection.

Our *Breakout* game can be customized as we want. Feel free to change the color defaults, the speed of the ball, or the number of rows of bricks.

However, GUI libraries are very limited, and more complex frameworks are required to achieve a wider range of capabilities. In the next chapter, we will introduce Cocos2d, a game framework that helps us with the development of our next game.

2
Cocos Invaders

In the previous chapter, we built a game with a **Graphical User Interface (GUI)** package called **Tkinter**. Since it is part of the Python's standard libraries, it was easy to set up the project and create the required widgets with a few lines of code. However, this kind of module falls short of providing the core functionality of game development beyond the 2D graphics.

The project covered in this chapter is developed with **cocos2d**. This framework has forks for different programming languages besides Python, such as C++, Objective-C, and JavaScript.

The game that we will develop is a variant of a classical game, *Space Invaders*. This arcade was a success of its time, and it has become part of the culture of video gaming.

In this two-dimensional game, the player must defeat waves of descending aliens by shooting them with a laser cannon, which can be moved horizontally and is protected by some defense bunkers. The enemy fire attempts to destroy the player's cannon, and it gradually damages the bunkers.

In our version, we will leave out the defense bunkers, and the game will look as follows:

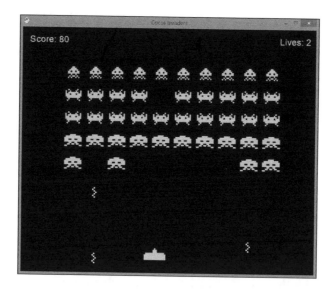

With this project, you will learn the following:

- The foundations of cocos2d
- How to work with sprites
- Processing input events
- Handling movements and collisions
- Complementing cocos2d with the Pyglet API

Installing cocos2d

In our previous game, we did not use any third-party package since Tkinter was part of the Python standard library. This is not the case with our new game framework, which must be downloaded and installed.

The **Python Package Index** (also called **PyPI**) is an official software repository of third-party packages, and thanks to package manager systems, this process becomes very straightforward. The pip is the packaging tool recommendation, and it is already included in the latest Python installations.

You can check whether `pip` is installed by running `pip --version`. The output indicates the version of `pip` and where it is located. This information may vary depending on your Python version and its installation directory:

```
$ pip --version
pip 6.0.8 from C:\Python34\lib\site-packages (python 3.4)
```

Since cocos2d is available on the PyPI, you can install it by running the following command:

```
$ pip install cocos2d
```

This command downloads and installs not only the cocos2d package but also its dependencies (**Pyglet** and **six**). Once run, the console output should print the progress and indicate that the installation was executed successfully. To verify that cocos2d is correctly installed, you can run this command:

```
$ python -c "import cocos; print(cocos.version)"
0.6.0
```

At the time of writing this book, the latest version of cocos2d is 0.6.0, so the output might be a greater version than this one.

> **The Python packaging ecosystem**
>
> Apart from `pip`, there are other packaging utilities, such as `easy_install` and `conda`. Each tool has different features and limitations, but in this book, we will stick with `pip` due to its ease of use and the fact that it is included in the latest Python installations by default.

Getting started with cocos2d

As with any other framework, cocos2d is composed of several modules and classes that implement different features. In order to develop applications with this API, we need to understand the following basic concepts:

- **Scene**: Each of the stages of your application is a scene. While your game may have many scenes, only one is active at any given point in time. The transition between scenes defines your game's workflow.

- **Layer**: Every sheet contained in a scene, whose overlay creates the final appearance of the scene, is called a layer. For instance, your game's main scene may have a background layer, an HUD layer with player information and scores, and an animation layer, where events and collisions between sprites are being processed.

- **Sprite**: This is a 2D image that can be manipulated though cocos2d actions, such as move, scale, or rotate. In our games, sprites will represent the player's character, enemies, and visual information, such as the number of lives left.

- **Director**: This is a shared object that initializes the main window and controls the current scene as well as the rest of the scenes that are on hold.

All of these classes except `Director` inherit from **CocosNode**. This class represents elements that are — or contain — nodes that get drawn, and it is part of the core of the library.

The functionality of this class covers parent-child relations, special placements, rendering, and scheduled actions. CocosNodes are also notified when they are added as a child of another node and when they are removed from their parent node.

This table has a summary of the most relevant members of this class:

Member	Description
`add(child, z=0, name=None)`	This adds a child. It raises an exception if the name already exists.
`remove(child)`	This removes a child given its name or the object. It raises an exception if the child is not on the list of children.
`kill()`	Removes itself from its parent.
`get_children()`	Returns a list of the children of the node, ordered by their *z* index.
`parent`	The parent node.
`position`	The position coordinates relative to the parent node.
`x`	The *x*-axis position coordinate.
`y`	The *y*-axis position coordinate.
`schedule(callback)`	This schedules a function to be called every frame.
`on_enter()`	This is called when added as a child while the parent is in the active scene, or if the scene goes active.
`on_exit()`	This is called when removed from its parent while the parent is in the active scene, or if the scene goes active.

With these definitions in mind, we can build our first cocos2d application. It will be a simple application in which the player must pick up four objects placed around the scene. The player character can be moved with the arrow keys, and there are neither menus nor display information.

The application will look like this:

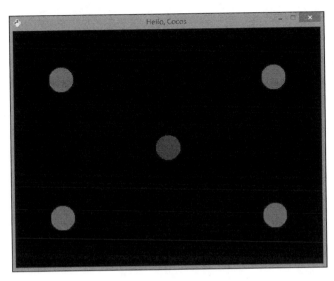

As can be seen, the functionality will be quite basic, since the purpose of this example is to familiarize yourself with the cocos2d modules.

Remember to save the script in the same directory as the `'ball.png'` image, since it is loaded by your game. The first iteration of our app contains the following code:

```
import cocos

class MainLayer(cocos.layer.Layer):
    def __init__(self):
        super(MainLayer, self).__init__()
        self.player = cocos.sprite.Sprite('ball.png')
        self.player.color = (0, 0, 255)
        self.player.position = (320, 240)
        self.add(self.player)

if __name__ == '__main__':
    cocos.director.director.init(caption='Hello, Cocos')
    layer = MainLayer()
    scene = cocos.scene.Scene(layer)
    cocos.director.director.run(scene)
```

First of all, we import the cocos module. We can import only the required modules separately (cocos.sprite, cocos.layer, cocos.scene, and cocos.director), which has the advantage of a quicker initialization. However, for this basic app, we will follow a simpler approach.

We have defined a custom layer by inheriting from the cocos.layer.Layer class. In this example, we call its parent __init__ method only, but as we will see later, there are other Layer subclasses that can be used for specialized functionality, such as ColorLayer and Menu.

The layer contains a single cocos.sprite.Sprite instance with the 'ball.png' image, which will represent the player character. The color attribute indicates the RGB color applied to the sprite image, represented as a tuple whose values range from 0 to 255. The position attribute, declared in the CocosNode class, sets the sprite's center coordinates. It is also possible to pass these values as keyword arguments to the __init__ method.

The main code block performs the following actions:

- Initializes the main window with the Director instance
- Instantiates our Layer subclass with the sprite
- Creates an empty scene that contains the layer
- Runs the Director main loop with the scene

Since director.init wraps the creation of a Pyglet window, the complete list of keyword parameters that can be passed to this method is available at the Pyglet Window API Reference.

For our cocos2d games, only a subset of these parameters will be used, and the most relevant keyword parameters are the following:

Parameter name	Description	Default value
fullscreen	A flag for creating the window that fills the entire screen	False
resizable	Indicates whether the window is resizable	False
vsync	Sync with the vertical retrace	True
width	Window width in pixels	640
height	Window height in pixels	480
caption	Window title (string)	
visible	Indicates whether the window is visible or not	True

Once we have set up the application, we extend its functionality by handling input events.

Handling user input

Each Layer is responsible for handling input events through the `is_event_handler` flag, which is set to `False` by default. If this flag is set to `True`, the Layer will receive input events and call the corresponding handler methods.

These are event listeners from the Layer class:

- `on_mouse_motion(x, y, dx, dy)`: The `(x, y)` are the physical coordinates of the mouse, and `(dx, dy)` is the distance vector covered by the mouse since the last call
- `on_mouse_press(x, y, buttons, modifiers)`: Just as in `on_mouse_motion`, `(x, y)` are the physical coordinates of the mouse, but this is called when a mouse button is pressed
- `on_mouse_drag(x, y, dx, dy, buttons, modifiers)`: A combination of `on_mouse_press` and `on_mouse_motion`, this is called when the mouse moves over with one or more buttons pressed
- `on_key_press(key, modifiers)`: This is called when a key is pressed
- `on_key_release(key, modifiers)`: This is called when a key is released

The `buttons` parameter is a bitwise OR of Pyglet button constants that are defined in the `pyglet.window.mouse` and `pyglet.window.key` modules for the `on_mouse` and `on_key` events, respectively. The `modifiers` parameter is a bitwise OR of the `pyglet.window.key` constants, such as *Shift*, *Option*, and *Alt*. You can find all the constants defined in this module at `https://pythonhosted.org/pyglet/api/pyglet.window.key-module.html`.

When you define one of these methods in your Layer subclass and the corresponding input event occurs, the method is called.

In this iteration of our sample game, we will print a message when a key is pressed or released:

 Note that since `Pyglet` is used internally for event handling, we need the `symbol_string` function from the `pyglet.window.key` module to decode the name of the key.

```
import cocos

from pyglet.window import key

class MainLayer(cocos.layer.Layer):
```

```
is_event_handler = True

def __init__(self):
    super(MainLayer, self).__init__()
    self.player = cocos.sprite.Sprite('ball.png')
    self.player.color = (0, 0, 255)
    self.player.position = (320, 240)
    self.add(self.player)

def on_key_press(self, k, m):
    print('Pressed', key.symbol_string(k))

def on_key_release(self, k, m):
    print('Released', key.symbol_string(k))
```

 We have omitted the if __name__ == '__main__' block, but remember to include it in your scripts in order to execute the application.

When you launch it, the keyboard events must be printed on the console. Our next step will be to reflect these events in the game state by modifying the sprite's position.

 The Pyglet event framework

Event handling is implemented in cocos2d with the Pyglet event framework. This event framework allows you to define emitters with a given event name (such as on_key_press) and register listeners over these events.

Remember that Pyglet is the multimedia library on which cocos2d relies, so we will see more usages of this API since major cocos2d applications use Pyglet modules.

Updating the scene

So far, our game only displays the same content, as objects are being modified. In a way similar to the Tkinter callback that was looping during the execution of our last game, we need to refresh our cocos2d application periodically.

This is achieved with the schedule method from the CocosNode class. It schedules a function that is called on every frame, and the first argument that this function receives is the elapsed time in seconds since the last clock tick.

While it is possible to pass additional arguments to this callback function, we will define a new method in the `MainLayer` class with the elapsed time parameter only:

```
import cocos

from collections import defaultdict
from pyglet.window import key

class MainLayer(cocos.layer.Layer):
    is_event_handler = True

    def __init__(self):
        super(MainLayer, self).__init__()
        self.player = cocos.sprite.Sprite('ball.png')
        self.player.color = (0, 0, 255)
        self.player.position = (320, 240)
        self.add(self.player)

        self.speed = 100.0
        self.pressed = defaultdict(int)
        self.schedule(self.update)

    def on_key_press(self, k, m):
        self.pressed[k] = 1

    def on_key_release(self, k, m):
        self.pressed[k] = 0

    def update(self, dt):
        x = self.pressed[key.RIGHT] - self.pressed[key.LEFT]
        y = self.pressed[key.UP] - self.pressed[key.DOWN]
        if x != 0 or y != 0:
            pos = self.player.position
            new_x = pos[0] + self.speed * x * dt
            new_y = pos[1] + self.speed * y * dt
            self.player.position = (new_x, new_y)
```

We have modified `on_key_press` and `on_key_release` so that they save the keystroke in `defaultdict`, a special dictionary from the `collections` module. This data structure returns the corresponding value if the key is present or the default value of the type if the key does not exist. In our case, since it is `defaultdict(int)`, the default value for the absent keys is `0`.

We have scheduled the update method, and for each frame, it checks the values of the pressed arrow keys. If the difference between these values is distinct to zero, the sprite is moved.

Processing collisions

In cocos2d, proximity and collisions among actors are calculated with an interface of the cocos.collision_model package called **CollisionManager**. This interface can be used to determine whether two objects are overlapping, or which objects are closer than a certain distance from a given object.

Actors should be added first to the set of objects that are managed by the collision manager, also called **known entities**. The set of managed objects is initially empty.

The CollisionManager interface is implemented by two classes:

- CollisionManagerBruteForce: This is a straightforward implementation. In it, all known entities are used to calculate proximity and collisions. It is intended for debugging purposes, and it does not scale if the set of known entities grows in size. It does not need any arguments in its initialization.

- CollisionManagerGrid: This divides the space into rectangular cells with a given width and height. When calculating the spatial relations between objects, it only considers the objects from the known entities that overlap the same cell. Its performance is better suited for a large number of known entities. The __init__ method requires the minimum and maximum coordinates of the space, the cell width, and the cell size. The recommended cell size is the maximum object width and height multiplied by 1.25. Note that as this factor increases its value, more objects overlap the same cell and the performance starts to degrade.

The reference of the CollisionManager methods that we are going to use in this chapter is the following:

Method	Description
add(obj)	Makes obj a known object
clear()	Empties the set of known objects
iter_colliding(obj)	Returns an iterator of objects colliding with obj
knows(obj)	This is true if obj is a known object

An object can be collided with if it has a member called **Cshape** and its value is an instance of `cocos.collision_model.Cshape`. There are two classes in cocos2d that inherit from Cshape:

- `CircleShape`: This uses a circle as the geometric space. When an instance is created, the center of the circle and its radius must be specified. Two circles collide if the Euclidean distance between their centers is less than the sum of their radius.
- `AARectShape`: This uses a rectangle as the geometric space. The rectangle is axis-aligned, which means that its sides are parallel to the x and y axes. This can be well suited if the actors do not rotate. Instead of the Euclidean distance, it uses the Manhattan distance to calculate a collision between two rectangles.

In our example, we will use circular shapes for our actors. In order to test the collision manager, four sprites are added to the Layer, and they will act as pickups—they will be destroyed when they collide with the player's sprite.

Besides, since `Cshape` requires a `cocos.euclid.Vector2` for the center coordinates, we will replace the tuples for the `Vector2` instances.

Before adding the collision manager, we define a new class to replace our sprites. The actors of our game share these attributes, so we will avoid code duplication:

```
import cocos
import cocos.collision_model as cm
import cocos.euclid as eu

from collections import defaultdict
from pyglet.window import key

class Actor(cocos.sprite.Sprite):
    def __init__(self, x, y, color):
        super(Actor, self).__init__('ball.png', color=color)
        self.position = pos = eu.Vector2(x, y)
        self.cshape = cm.CircleShape(pos, self.width/2)
```

Now that we have this base class, we can add these objects with the required `cshape` member. The collision manager implementation that we will use in all our applications is `CollisionManagerGrid`, since the brute-force implementation is only intended for reference and debugging:

```
class MainLayer(cocos.layer.Layer):
```

```
        is_event_handler = True

    def __init__(self):
        super(MainLayer, self).__init__()
        self.player = Actor(320, 240, (0, 0, 255))
        self.add(self.player)
        for pos in [(100,100), (540,380),\
                (540,100), (100,380)]:
            self.add(Actor(pos[0], pos[1], (255, 0, 0)))

        cell = self.player.width * 1.25
        self.collman = cm.CollisionManagerGrid(0, 640, 0, 480,
                                               cell, cell)
        self.speed = 100.0
        self.pressed = defaultdict(int)
        self.schedule(self.update)

    def on_key_press(self, k, m):
        self.pressed[k] = 1

    def on_key_release(self, k, m):
        self.pressed[k] = 0
```

Now the update method must perform the following steps in order to be able to detect collisions of moving objects: clear the collision manager, add the actors to the set of known entities, and iterate over the objects' collisions:

```
    def update(self, dt):
        self.collman.clear()
        for _, node in self.children:
            self.collman.add(node)
        for other in self.collman.iter_colliding(self.player):
            self.remove(other)

        x = self.pressed[key.RIGHT] - self.pressed[key.LEFT]
        y = self.pressed[key.UP] - self.pressed[key.DOWN]
        if x != 0 or y != 0:
            pos = self.player.position
            new_x = pos[0] + self.speed * x * dt
            new_y = pos[1] + self.speed * y * dt
            self.player.position = (new_x, new_y)
            self.player.cshape.center = self.player.position
```

Note the statement in which the `cshape` center of the player sprite is updated with the new position. Without this line, the collision manager will not detect any collision between the player and the pickups, since the entity center will always be in the initial position.

In the `chapter2_01.py` script, you can find the complete code. For this application, we only needed a single sprite. However, most games use several images to represent different game characters and their animations.

In the next section, we will see the sprites that our *Space Invaders* game will have.

Creating game assets

We will need a few basic images for our cocos2d sprites. They will be the visual representations of the player's cannon and the different types of aliens.

The following image shows how these sprites can be drawn with an image editor program, with the help of a grid:

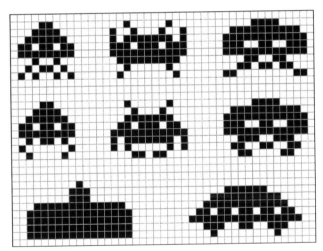

Unfortunately, the usage of image manipulation tools is beyond the scope of this book. There is a wide variety in these programs, and for basic sprites (such as the ones shown in the previous image), you can use MS Paint on Windows systems.

Under the `img` folder, you can find the different images that we will use in our game. Feel free to edit them and change their colors. However, do not modify their size as it is used to determine the width and the height of the Sprite and its Cshape member.

Creating your own "pixel art"

There are more advanced applications that can be run on any platform. This is the case of GIMP, an open source program that is part of the GNU project. The sprites used in this chapter have been drawn with GIMP 2, the current version.

You can download it for free from http://www.gimp.org/downloads/.

Space Invaders design

Before writing our game with cocos2d, we should consider which actors we need to model in order to represent our game entities. In our *Space Invaders* version, we will use the following classes:

- PlayerCannon: This is the character controlled by the player. The spacebar is used to shoot, and the horizontal movement is controlled with the right and left arrow keys.

- Alien: Each one of the descending enemies, with different looks and scores depending on the alien type.

- AlienColumn: There are columns of five aliens into which every group of aliens is divided.

- AlienGroup: A whole group of enemies. It moves horizontally or descends uniformly.

- Shoot: A small projectile launched by the enemies towards the player character.

- PlayerShoot: A Shoot subclass. It is launched by the player rather than the alien group.

Apart from these classes, we need a custom Layer for the game logic, which will be named GameLayer, and a base class for the logic that is shared among the actors—similar to the GameObject class from our previous game.

We will call it **Actor**, as we did in our previous cocos2d application. In fact, it is quite similar to that one, except that this implementation adds the definition of two methods: update and collide. They will be called when our game loop updates the position of the nodes and when a known entity hits the actor, respectively.

This module is new, apart from the code we saw in the previous section, and it will contain the following code:

```
import cocos.sprite
import cocos.collision_model as cm
import cocos.euclid as eu

class Actor(cocos.sprite.Sprite):
    def __init__(self, image, x, y):
        super(Actor, self).__init__(image)
        self.position = eu.Vector2(x, y)
        self.cshape = cm.AARectShape(self.position,
                                     self.width * 0.5,
                                     self.height * 0.5)

    def move(self, offset):
        self.position += offset
        self.cshape.center += offset

    def update(self, elapsed):
        pass

    def collide(self, other):
        pass
```

The `PlayerCannon`, `Alien`, `Shoot`, and `PlayerShoot` classes will extend from this class. Therefore, with this little piece of code, we have set up the interface for collision detection and the movements of all our game objects.

The PlayerCannon and GameLayer classes

As we saw earlier, `PlayerCannon` is one of our game actors. It must respond to the left and right keystrokes to control the horizontal movement of the sprite, and the object is destroyed if an enemy's shot hits it.

We will implement this by overriding both `update` and `collide`:

```
from collections import defaultdict
from pyglet.window import key

class PlayerCannon(Actor):
```

```
KEYS_PRESSED = defaultdict(int)

def __init__(self, x, y):
    super(PlayerCannon, self).__init__('img/cannon.png', x, y)
    self.speed = eu.Vector2(200, 0)

def update(self, elapsed):
    pressed = PlayerCannon.KEYS_PRESSED
    movement = pressed[key.RIGHT] - pressed[key.LEFT]
    w = self.width * 0.5
    if movement != 0 and w <= self.x <= self.parent.width - w:
        self.move(self.speed * movement * elapsed)

def collide(self, other):
    other.kill()
    self.kill()
```

To determine whether a key is pressed or not, we have defined `defaultdict`, as in our basic cocos2d application. In this case, it is a class attribute of `PlayerCannon`. The horizontal movement is limited so that the character cannot leave the collision manager grid.

The `GameLayer` class will be the main layer of our game, and it will be responsible for doing the following:

- Keeping track of the number of player lives left and the current score
- Handling input key events by setting its `is_event_handler` flag to `true`
- Creating the game actors and adding them as child nodes
- Running the game loop by executing a scheduled function for each frame where the collisions are processed and the object positions are updated

Its initial implementation is the following:

```
import cocos.layer

class GameLayer(cocos.layer.Layer):
    is_event_handler = True

    def on_key_press(self, k, _):
        PlayerCannon.KEYS_PRESSED[k] = 1

    def on_key_release(self, k, _):
```

```
            PlayerCannon.KEYS_PRESSED[k] = 0

    def __init__(self):
        super(GameLayer, self).__init__()
        w, h = cocos.director.director.get_window_size()
        self.width = w
        self.height = h
        self.lives = 3
        self.score = 0
        self.update_score()
        self.create_player()
        self.create_alien_group(100, 300)
        cell = 1.25 * 50
        self.collman = cm.CollisionManagerGrid(0, w, 0, h,
                                                cell, cell)
        self.schedule(self.update)
```

The `create_player` method adds a `PlayerCannon` in the center of the screen. It will be called each time the player character needs to be respawned, while `update_score` increments the score by adding the points for each alien that is destroyed. The default value of the `score=0` argument in the method signature means that if no arguments are passed, the argument's value will be `0`:

```
    def create_player(self):
        self.player = PlayerCannon(self.width * 0.5, 50)
        self.add(self.player)

    def update_score(self, score=0):
        self.score += score
```

The `create_alien_group` method initializes the rows of descending aliens. Since the required classes have not been implemented yet, we will leave it with the `pass` statement for now:

```
    def create_alien_group(self, x, y):
        pass
```

The `update` method is a callback that will be scheduled to be executed for each frame:

```
    def update(self, dt):
        self.collman.clear()
        for _, node in self.children:
            self.collman.add(node)
```

```
        if not self.collman.knows(node):
            self.remove(node)

    for _, node in self.children:
        node.update(dt)
```

We did a small trick here. As we saw in the `CollisionManager` reference, the `knows` method checks whether an object is in the set of known entities—which should be always true since all of the layer's children have been added.

However, when an object is outside of the surface covered by the collision manager, it does not overlap with any cell of the grid and it is considered to be "not known." In this way, objects that move out of this area are automatically removed:

```
def collide(self, node):
    if node is not None:
        for other in self.collman.iter_colliding(node):
            node.collide(other)
            return True
    return False
```

Finally, the `collide` method encapsulates the call to `iter_colliding` and checks whether the node is a reference to a valid object—the `PlayerShoot` instance can be `None` if there is no current shoot.

As usual, we write the main block for the moment when our script is run as the main module:

```
if __name__ == '__main__':
    cocos.director.director.init(caption='Cocos Invaders',
                                 width=800, height=650)
    game_layer = GameLayer()
    main_scene = cocos.scene.Scene(game_layer)
    cocos.director.director.run(main_scene)
```

Invaders!

There are three classes used to represent our invaders: `Alien`, `AlienColumn`, and `AlienGroup`.

Out of these classes, only `Alien` inherits from `Actor` because it is the only entity that is drawn and collides with other objects. Instead of a static image, the sprite will be a basic animation wherein each image will be shown for 0.5 seconds. This is achieved by loading an `ImageGrid` and creating an `Animation` from this sprite grid. Since these classes belong to the `pyglet.image` module, we need to import them first.

Another function of our aliens will be notifying its column that the object has been removed. Thanks to this, the column of aliens knows what the bottom one is and starts shooting from its position.

You learned from the CocosNode reference that the `on_exit` method is called when a node is removed, so you will be overriding it to inform its corresponding column. Note that a reference to the column is passed to the `__init__` method. We could have implemented the same functionality with a `Pyglet` event handler mechanism, but that would require pushing the handlers to every `Alien` instance:

```python
from pyglet.image import load, ImageGrid, Animation

class Alien(Actor):
    def load_animation(imgage):
        seq = ImageGrid(load(imgage), 2, 1)
        return Animation.from_image_sequence(seq, 0.5)

    TYPES = {
        '1': (load_animation('img/alien1.png'), 40),
        '2': (load_animation('img/alien2.png'), 20),
        '3': (load_animation('img/alien3.png'), 10)
    }

    def from_type(x, y, alien_type, column):
        animation, score = Alien.TYPES[alien_type]
        return Alien(animation, x, y, score, column)

    def __init__(self, img, x, y, score, column=None):
        super(Alien, self).__init__(img, x, y)
        self.score = score
        self.column = column

    def on_exit(self):
        super(Alien, self).on_exit()
        if self.column:
            self.column.remove(self)
```

The TYPES class attribute help us load the animations only once, at the beginning of the game. The `score` is the number of points earned when the enemy is destroyed, while the `column` attribute contains a reference to the column to which the alien belongs.

The `AlienColumn` class is responsible for instantiating the columns of aliens with a given pattern, like this:

Since we have defined the `Alien.from_type` utility method, we call it in the proper order to place each type of alien, as seen in the previous figure:

```
class AlienColumn(object):
    def __init__(self, x, y):
        alien_types = enumerate(['3', '3', '2', '2', '1'])
        self.aliens = [Alien.from_type(x, y+i*60, alien, self)
                       for i, alien in alien_types]

    def remove(self, alien):
        self.aliens.remove(alien)

    def shoot(self): pass
```

The `should_turn` method checks whether, given the current direction, the column has reached the side of the screen or not. It will return `False` if there are no aliens left in the column:

```
    def should_turn(self, d):
        if len(self.aliens) == 0:
            return False
        alien = self.aliens[0]
        x, width = alien.x, alien.parent.width
        return x >= width - 50 and d == 1 or x <= 50
        and d == -1
```

All the `AlienColumn` instances form the `AlienGroup`. It is moved uniformly, and it delegates the shooting logic to each column. This movement is implemented with the speed and `direction` object attributes.

While the alien group is being updated, it sums the elapsed times between frames. When a certain period has elapsed, the whole group is moved down or laterally. The direction will depend on whether any column has reached the lateral sides or not:

```python
class AlienGroup(object):
    def __init__(self, x, y):
        self.columns = [AlienColumn(x + i * 60, y)
                            for i in range(10)]
        self.speed = eu.Vector2(10, 0)
        self.direction = 1
        self.elapsed = 0.0
        self.period = 1.0

    def update(self, elapsed):
        self.elapsed += elapsed
        while self.elapsed >= self.period:
            self.elapsed -= self.period
            offset = self.direction * self.speed
            if self.side_reached():
                self.direction *= -1
                offset = eu.Vector2(0, -10)
            for alien in self:
                alien.move(offset)

    def side_reached(self):
        return any(map(lambda c: c.should_turn(self.direction),
                        self.columns))

    def __iter__(self):
        for column in self.columns:
            for alien in column.aliens:
                yield alien
```

Here, we also define a __iter__ method, which is a special method that is invoked when you iterate over an object. In this way, we can call for alien in alien_group in the rest of our code.

Now that we have implemented the logic of our enemies and the movement of the whole group, we can add its instantiation to the GameLayer class:

```python
    def create_alien_group(self, x, y):
        self.alien_group = AlienGroup(x, y)
        for alien in self.alien_group:
            self.add(alien)
```

This creates a new alien group and adds all the enemies to the layer as child nodes. The `chapter2_02.py` script contains the code that we have written so far, and its execution will look like this:

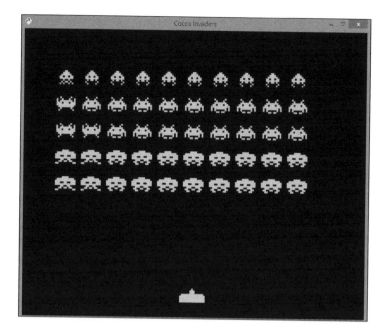

Shoot'em up!

The `Shoot` actor, by itself, is quite basic; it only requires a `speed` attribute and overrides the `update` method so that the object is moved by the distance determined by this speed and the elapsed time between frames:

```
class Shoot(Actor):
    def __init__(self, x, y, img='img/shoot.png'):
        super(Shoot, self).__init__(img, x, y)
        self.speed = eu.Vector2(0, -400)

    def update(self, elapsed):
        self.move(self.speed * elapsed)
```

The `PlayerShoot` class requires a bit more logic, since the player cannot shoot until the previous beam has hit an enemy or reached the end of the screen.

As we want to avoid global variables, we will use a class attribute to hold the reference to the current shot. When the shot leaves the scene, this reference will be set to None again.

We will override the collide method from the Actor class so that both the beam and the alien are destroyed when a collision occurs. This is done by calling the kill method defined in the Sprite class. It internally removes the CocosNode from its parent:

```
class PlayerShoot(Shoot):
    INSTANCE = None

    def __init__(self, x, y):
        super(PlayerShoot, self).__init__(x, y,
        'img/laser.png')
        self.speed *= -1
        PlayerShoot.INSTANCE = self

    def collide(self, other):
        if isinstance(other, Alien):
            self.parent.update_score(other.score)
            other.kill()
            self.kill()

    def on_exit(self):
        super(PlayerShoot, self).on_exit()
        PlayerShoot.INSTANCE = None
```

With this class, we can add this functionality to the update method of PlayerCannon:

```
    def update(self, elapsed):
        pressed = PlayerCannon.KEYS_PRESSED
        space_pressed = pressed[key.SPACE] == 1
        if PlayerShoot.INSTANCE is None and space_pressed:
            self.parent.add(PlayerShoot(self.x, self.y + 50))

        movement = pressed[key.RIGHT] - pressed[key.LEFT]
        if movement != 0:
            self.move(self.speed * movement * elapsed)
```

The shoot method in AlienColumn — which we left unimplemented — can be modified with our new Shoot class.

To randomly shoot a new beam, we will call `random.random()`, which returns a random float between the semi-open range of `(0.0, 1.0)`. We will set a low probability. This is because this function will be called several times per second. The `random` module is part of the Python standard library, so you can start playing around with it by adding the `import` random statement at the beginning of the script:

```
def shoot(self):
    if random.random() < 0.001 and len(self.aliens) > 0:
        pos = self.aliens[0].position
        return Shoot(pos[0], pos[1] - 50)
    return None
```

Now the `update` method of the `GameLayer` class can calculate which objects collide with the cannon and the player's current shot, as well as randomly shoot from the alien columns:

```
def update(self, dt):
    self.collman.clear()
    for _, node in self.children:
        self.collman.add(node)
        if not self.collman.knows(node):
            self.remove(node)

    self.collide(PlayerShoot.INSTANCE)
    if self.collide(self.player):
        self.respawn_player()
    for column in self.alien_group.columns:
        shoot = column.shoot()
        if shoot is not None:
            self.add(shoot)

    for _, node in self.children:
        node.update(dt)
    self.alien_group.update(dt)
```

Here, `respawn_player()` decrements the number of lives, and it unschedules `update` if there are no lives left. This stops the main loop and represents the game over situation:

```
def respawn_player(self):
    self.lives -= 1
    if self.lives < 0:
```

```
                self.unschedule(self.update)
        else:
                self.create_player()
```

In this iteration, the game we have built is very similar to the final version. The playable character can be moved with the arrow keys and is able to shoot. The enemies move uniformly, and the lower alien of each row can shoot as well. The code for this implementation can be found in the `chapter2_03.py` script.

Now, the only detail left is displaying the game information: the current score and the number of lives left.

Adding an HUD

Our "heads-up display" will be a new Layer that will be drawn over our `GameLayer`:

```python
class HUD(cocos.layer.Layer):
    def __init__(self):
        super(HUD, self).__init__()
        w, h = cocos.director.director.get_window_size()
        self.score_text = cocos.text.Label('', font_size=18)
        self.score_text.position = (20, h - 40)
        self.lives_text = cocos.text.Label('', font_size=18)
        self.lives_text.position = (w - 100, h - 40)
        self.add(self.score_text)
        self.add(self.lives_text)

    def update_score(self, score):
        self.score_text.element.text = 'Score: %s' % score

    def update_lives(self, lives):
        self.lives_text.element.text = 'Lives: %s' % lives

    def show_game_over(self):
        w, h = cocos.director.director.get_window_size()
        game_over = cocos.text.Label('Game Over', font_size=50,
                                     anchor_x='center',
                                     anchor_y='center')
        game_over.position = w * 0.5, h * 0.5
        self.add(game_over)
```

Our `GameLayer` will hold a reference to the HUD layer, and its methods will be modified so that they can call the HUD directly:

```
def __init__(self, hud):
    super(GameLayer, self).__init__()
    w, h = cocos.director.director.get_window_size()
    self.hud = hud
    self.width = w
    self.height = h
    # ...
```

The `hud` attribute will be used when the player needs to be respawned and when the score is updated:

```
def create_player(self):
    self.player = PlayerCannon(self.width * 0.5, 50)
    self.add(self.player)
    self.hud.update_lives(self.lives)

def respawn_player(self):
    self.lives -= 1
    if self.lives < 0:
        self.unschedule(self.update)
        self.hud.show_game_over()
    else:
        self.create_player()

def update_score(self, score=0):
    self.score += score
    self.hud.update_score(self.score)
```

The main block should also be modified to create the scene with the two layers. Here, we pass the z index to indicate the ordering of the children layers:

```
if __name__ == '__main__':
    cocos.director.director.init(caption='Cocos Invaders',
                                 width=800, height=650)
    main_scene = cocos.scene.Scene()
    hud_layer = HUD()
    main_scene.add(hud_layer, z=1)
    game_layer = GameLayer(hud_layer)
    main_scene.add(game_layer, z=0)
    cocos.director.director.run(main_scene)
```

Extra feature – the mystery ship

To complete our game, we will add a final ingredient: the mystery ship that randomly appears at the top of the screen:

```
class MysteryShip(Alien):
    SCORES = [10, 50, 100, 200]

    def __init__(self, x, y):
        score = random.choice(MysteryShip.SCORES)
        super(MysteryShip, self).__init__('img/alien4.png', x, y,
                                          score)
        self.speed = eu.Vector2(150, 0)

    def update(self, elapsed):
        self.move(self.speed * elapsed)
```

In an approach similar to the shooting logic of our enemies, we will randomly add this alien to our scheduled function:

```
def update(self, dt):
    self.collman.clear()
    # ...
    self.alien_group.update(dt)

    if random.random() < 0.001:
        self.add(MysteryShip(50, self.height - 50))
```

You can find the complete implementation of this game in the `chapter2_04.py` script. Enjoy your first cocos2d game!

Summary

In this chapter, we introduced cocos2d and its most relevant modules. We developed our first application to get started with the library, and later we built a simplified version of *Space Invaders*.

This version can be extended by adding defense bunkers or more random values to the possible scores of the mystery ship. Besides, if you want to change the visual appearance of the invaders, you can edit the sprites and create your own enemies!

In the next chapter, we will develop a complete tower defense game, with transitions between scenes, enhanced display information, and complex menus.

3
Building a Tower Defense Game

In the previous chapter, you learned the fundamentals of cocos2d, and now you are able to develop a basic game with this library. However, most games use more than a single scene, and their complexity it is not limited to collisions and input detection.

With our next game, we will dive into the **cocos2d** modules that provide us the advanced functionality we are looking for: menus, transitions, scheduled actions, and an efficient way of storing level graphics.

In this chapter, we will cover these topics:

- How to manipulate sprites with cocos2d actions
- Using tile maps as background layers
- Animated transitions between game scenes
- How to create scenes that act as menus and cut scenes
- Building a full-fledged cocos2d application with all the ingredients you have learned so far

The tower defense gameplay

The genre of tower defense challenges the player to stop enemy characters from reaching a certain position by placing strategically different towers so that they can defeat the enemies before they arrive at that point. The towers shoot autonomously towards the enemies that are within their firing range. The game is over when a concrete number of enemies reach the end point.

In our version, the scenario will be a meandering road in the desert, and we have to protect a bunker that is placed at the end of this road, as shown in the following screenshot. At the far end, enemy tanks will be spawning randomly, and we must place turrets that destroy them before they reach our bunker. The turrets can be placed in specific slots, and each turret spends part of our limited resources.

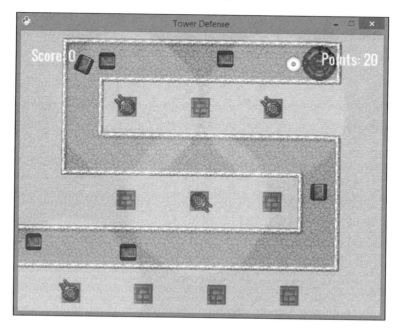

Cocos2d actions

In our previous game, we manipulated our sprites directly through their members, especially the `position` attribute. The game loop updated each actor with the elapsed time from the previous frame.

However, our tower defense game will be based mainly on cocos2d **actions**, which are orders to modify object attributes such as the position, rotation, or scale. They are executed by calling the `do()` method of the `CocosNode` class. Therefore, any **sprite**, **layer**, or **scene** can be a valid target of an action.

The actions that we will cover in this section can be divided into two main groups: **interval actions** and **instant actions**.

Interval actions

These actions have a duration, and their execution ends after that certain duration. For instance, if we want to move a sprite to a certain position, we do not want it to happen immediately but last a fixed amount of time, giving the impression that it moves with a determined speed. This can be achieved with the `MoveTo` action:

```
import cocos
import cocos.actions as ac

if __name__ == '__main__':
    cocos.director.director.init(caption='Actions 101')

    layer = cocos.layer.Layer()
    sprite = cocos.sprite.Sprite('tank.png', position=(200, 200))
    sprite.do(ac.MoveTo((250, 300), 3))
    layer.add(sprite)

    scene = cocos.scene.Scene(layer)
    cocos.director.director.run(scene)
```

In this sample, we move our tank sprite, initially placed at position `(200, 200)`, to position `(250, 300)`. The second argument of `MoveTo` indicates the duration, which is 3 seconds. If we wanted to use a relative offset instead of the absolute coordinates, we could have used the `MoveBy` action. The equivalent in this example would be `MoveBy((50, 100), 3)`.

Another common action is rotating a node, and for this purpose, cocos2d offers the `RotateBy` and `RotateTo` actions, which take the angle in degrees and the duration in seconds:

```
# ...
sprite = cocos.sprite.Sprite('tank.png', position=(200, 200))
sprite.do(ac.RotateBy(180, 5)) # Rotate 180 degrees in 5 sec
```

Like `MoveTo` and `MoveBy`, the difference between `RotateTo` and `RotateBy` is the use of absolute and relative rotations.

The math module

The Python standard library contains a module with commonly used mathematical functions. Since cocos2d works with degrees for rotation actions, the `math.degrees(radians)` and `math.radians(degrees)` conversion utilities included in the `math` module can be extremely useful.

See the entire functionality provided by this module at `https://docs.python.org/3.4/library/math.html`.

The complete reference of instant actions included in the `cocos.actions.interval_actions` module is the following:

Interval action	Description
Lerp	Interpolates between values for a specified attribute
MoveTo	Moves the target to the position (x, y)
MoveBy	Moves the target by an offset of (x, y)
JumpTo	Moves the target to a position simulating a jump movement
JumpBy	Moves the target simulating a jump movement
Bezier	Moves the target through a Bézier path
Blink	Blinks the target by hiding and showing it a number of times
RotateTo	Rotates the target to a certain angle
RotateBy	Rotates a target clockwise by a number of degrees
ScaleTo	Scales the target to a zoom factor
ScaleBy	Scales the target by a zoom factor
FadeOut	Fades out the target by modifying its opacity attribute
FadeIn	Fades in the target by modifying its opacity attribute
FadeTo	Fades the target to a specific alpha value
Delay	Delays the action by a certain number of seconds
RandomDelay	Delays the action randomly between a minimum value and a maximum value of seconds

Instant actions

We have just introduced interval actions. These are applied over a duration of time. Now we will cover instant actions, which are applied immediately to the CocosNode instance. Actually, they are internally implemented as interval actions with zero duration. One example of an instant action is `CallFunc`, which invokes a function when the action is executed:

```
import cocos.actions as ac

def update_score():
    print('Updating the score...')

sprite = cocos.sprite.Sprite('tank.png', position=(200, 200))
sprite.do(ac.CallFunc(update_score))
```

As we will see later, this action will be handy when we want to call a specific function during a sequence of actions.

Note that the `update_score` argument in the last line is not followed by `()`. This is a subtle but important difference; it means that we are creating `CallFunc` with a reference to the `update_score` function, instead of actually invoking it.

The following table contains all the actions defined in the `cocos.actions.instant_actions` module:

Instant action	Description
Place	Places the target in the position *(x, y)*
CallFunc	Calls a function
CallFuncS	Calls a function with the target as the first argument
Hide	Hides the target by setting its visibility to `False`
Show	Shows the target by setting its visibility to `True`
ToggleVisibility	Toggles the visibility of the target

Combining actions

By now, you know how to apply actions separately, but you need to combine them in order to achieve a more complex behavior.

The `Action` class, defined in the `cocos.actions.base_actions` module, is the base class that `InstantAction` and `IntervalAction` inherit from. It implements the `__add__` special method, which is called internally when we use the + operator.

This operator creates a sequence of actions that are applied serially to the target:

```
sprite = cocos.sprite.Sprite('tank.png', position=(200, 200))
sprite.do(ac.MoveBy((80, 0), 3) + ac.Delay(1) + \
          ac.CallFunc(sprite.kill))
```

This snippet moves our tank 80 pixels to the right in 3 seconds. It stands for 1 second, and finally, it is removed by calling the `kill()` method.

Apart from `__add__`, the `__or__` special method is also overridden. It is invoked when the | operator is used and runs the actions in parallel:

```
sprite = cocos.sprite.Sprite('tank.png', position=(200, 200))
sprite.do(ac.MoveTo((500, 150), 3) | ac.RotateBy(90, 2))
```

This moves the sprite to the `(500, 150)` position in 3 seconds, and during the first 2 seconds, it rotates 90 degrees clockwise.

The __add__ and __or__ special methods can be combined to produce a sequence of actions that run both in parallel and sequentially:

```
sprite = cocos.sprite.Sprite('tank.png', position=(200, 200))
sprite.do((ac.MoveTo((500, 150), 3) | ac.RotateBy(90, 2)) + \
          ac.CallFunc(sprite.kill))
```

This example performs combined movement and rotation as the previous one, but when the parallel actions are done, it removes the sprite.

Python's special methods

Cocos2d implements action sequences by emulating numeric operators, but these could have been implemented with normal methods. In programing, this kind of shortcut offered by a language is called **syntactic sugar**, and it succinctly expresses a functionality that can also be implemented in a more verbose manner.

Custom actions

We have a full list of actions included in the library, but what if none of these actions perform the visual effect that we desire and we want to define a new action?

We can create instant or interval actions by extending the corresponding class. For our game, we want an action that indicates visually that an enemy tank has been hit by applying a red filter to the tank, and it should gradually return to the original color.

In this case, we define an `IntervalAction` subclass called `Hit`, keeping in mind that the following steps will be performed internally by cocos2d:

- The `init(*args, **kwargs)` is called. One of these keyword arguments should be the duration of the action, so you can set it as your duration attribute. Do not confuse this with the `__init__` special method.
- A copy of the instance is made; usually, this should not have any side effect.
- The `start()` is called. From here, the `self.target` attribute can be used.
- The `update(t)` is called several times, where t is the time in the (0, 1) range.
- Then, `update(1)` is called.
- The `stop()` is called.

It is not necessary to override all of these methods, but only those that are required to implement your action. For instance, we only need to store the duration and update the color of the sprite depending on the elapsed time, t:

```
class Hit(ac.IntervalAction):
    def init(self, duration=0.5):
        self.duration = duration

    def update(self, t):
        self.target.color = (255, 255 * t, 255 * t)
```

When update(0) is invoked, the sprite's color will be (255, 0, 0), which looks as if a red filter is being applied to the image. The red tone will decrease as the elapsed time, t, rises monotonically.

Since we know that update(1) will be called, the final color of the target will be (255, 255, 255), and there is no need to reset the initial color of the sprite.

The following snippet shows how this new action can be used:

```
sprite = cocos.sprite.Sprite('tank.png', position=(200, 200))
sprite.do(ac.MoveBy((100,0),3) + Hit() + ac.MoveBy((50,0),2))
```

In the Chapter3_01.py script, you can see this snippet with all of the usual code required to run the scene.

Adding a main menu

The *Space Invaders* version that we developed in the previous chapter starts a new game as soon as the application is loaded. In most games, an initial screen is displayed and the player can choose between different options apart from starting a new game, such as changing the default controls or taking a look at the high scores.

The cocos.menu cocos2d module offers a Layer subclass named **Menu**, which serves exactly this purpose. By extending it, you can override its __init__ method and set the style of the title, the menu items, and the selected menu item.

These items are represented as a list of MenuItem instances. Once this list is instantiated, you can call the create_menu method, which builds the final menu with the actions that are executed when a menu item is selected.

While the basic `MenuItem` only displays a static label, there are several `MenuItem` subclasses for distinct input modes:

- `ToggleMenuItem`: Toggles a Boolean option
- `MultipleMenuItem`: Switches between multiple values
- `EntryMenuItem`: This is the menu item for entering a text input
- `ImageMenuItem`: Shows a selectable image instead of a text label
- `ColorMenuItem`: This is the menu item for selecting a color

All of these classes except `ImageMenuItem` invoke a callback function when its value changes to this new value as the first argument.

A typical usage could be the following:

```
import cocos
from cocos.menu import *
import pyglet.app

class MainMenu(Menu):
    def __init__(self):
        super(MainMenu, self).__init__('Sample menu')
        self.font_title['font_name'] = 'Times New Roman'
        self.font_title['font_size'] = 60
        self.font_title['bold'] = True
        self.font_item['font_name'] = 'Times New Roman'
        self.font_item_selected['font_name'] = \
            'Times New Roman'

        self.difficulty = ['Easy', 'Normal', 'Hard']
        m1 = MenuItem('New Game', self.start_game)
        m2 = EntryMenuItem('Player name:', self.set_player_name,
                           'John Doe', max_length=10)
        m3 = MultipleMenuItem('Difficulty: ',
        self.set_difficulty,
        self.difficulty)
        m4 = ToggleMenuItem('Show FPS: ', self.show_fps, False)
        m5 = MenuItem('Quit', pyglet.app.exit)
        self.create_menu([m1, m2, m3, m4, m5],
                         shake(), shake_back())
```

When `self.create_menu` is called, we can pass a cocos2d action that is applied when a menu item is activated and when it is deactivated. The `cocos.menu` module includes a few actions, and we imported the `shake()` and `shake_back()` actions, which perform a little shake movement at the current menu item and return to the original style when the option is deselected, respectively.

The rest of the code has been omitted for brevity; you can find the complete script in `Chapter3_02.py` with the class methods that are called when a menu item is activated. Note the reference to the `pyglet.app.exit` function, which finalizes the cocos2d application.

With just a few lines of code, we have built a menu where the player can input their name, set the game difficulty, and toggle the FPS display. The menu items can be selected with the arrow keys or the mouse pointer.

This is the type of main menu we are looking for for our tower defense game. Since this is only one layer, we can later add a background layer that improves the visual appearance of the menu.

Now that you have understood the menu API, let's move on to the design of the main scene.

Tile maps

The technique of tile maps became a successful approach to storing large amounts of information about game worlds with small, reusable pieces of graphics. In 2D games, tile maps are represented by a two-dimensional matrix that references to a tile object. This object contains the required data about each cell of the terrain.

The initial sheet used by the tile map contains the "building blocks" of our scenario, and it looks like what is shown in the following screenshot:

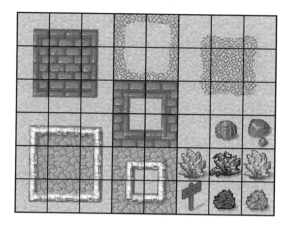

Starting from this simple image, we can build a grid map in which each cell is one of the squares the sheet is divided into.

Tiled Map Editor

We will use **Tiled Map Editor**, a useful tool for manipulating tiled maps. It can be downloaded for free from `http://www.mapeditor.org/`, and it can be run on most operating systems, including Windows and Mac OS.

This software is also well-suited for level design, since you can edit and visualize the resulting world in a simple way.

Once we have installed and launched the program, we can load the image that we will use for our tile map. For this game, we have used a PNG image that is already bundled with the Map Editor installation.

In the menu bar, go to **File | New...** to create a new map. When a new map is created, you will be prompted for some basic information, such as the map orientation, map size, size of the pattern, and spacing between the cells. In our game, we will use an orthogonal map of 640 x 480 pixels and 32 x 32 pixels for each cell, as shown in the following screenshot:

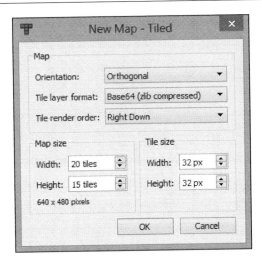

Now go to **Map** | **New Tileset...**, enter the name map0, and load the tmw_desert_ spacing.png image from the examples folder, as shown in this screenshot:

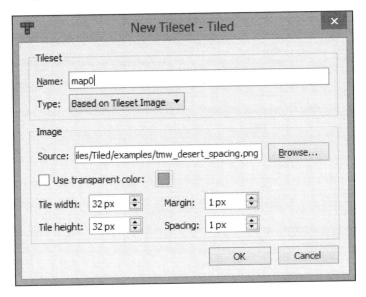

You can use the tiles shown in the **Tileset** view to draw a map like this one:

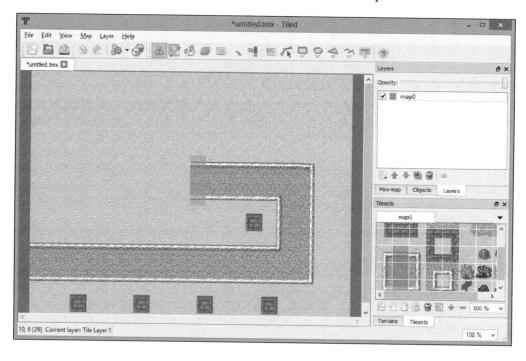

Once the map is drawn, we can save it in several file formats, such as CSV, JSON, or TXT. We will choose the **TMX format**, which is an XML file that can be loaded by cocos2d. Go to **File | Save as...** to store the tiled map with this format.

Loading tiles

Thanks to the `cocos.tiles` module, we can load our tile maps as layers and manipulate them like any other `CocosNode` instance. If our TMX file and the corresponding PNG image are stored in the `assets` folder, and the name of the map we want to load is `'map0'`, this would be the code necessary to load it:

```
import cocos

tmx_file = cocos.tiles.load('assets/tower_defense.tmx')
my_map = tmx_file('map0')
my_map.set_view(0, 0, my_map.px_width, my_map.px_height)
scene = cocos.scene.Scene(my_map)
```

The scenario definition

Once we have loaded the tile map, we need to link the resulting image with the game information. Our scenario class should contain the following:

- The positions where the turrets can be placed
- The position of the bunker
- The initial position for enemy spawning
- The path that the enemies must follow to reach the bunker

In the following screenshot, we can see this data overlaid on top of our TMX map:

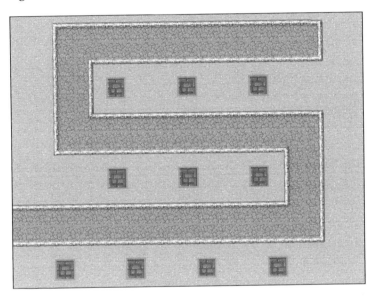

The rectangles represent the slots in which the player can place the turrets. The scenario stores only the centers of these squares, because the game layer will translate these positions into clickable squares.

The lines over the road represent the path that the enemy tanks must follow. This movement will be implemented by chaining the MoveBy and RotateBy actions. We will define two constants for rotation toward the left or the right, and an auxiliary function that returns a MoveBy action whose duration makes the enemies move uniformly:

```
import cocos.actions as ac

RIGHT = ac.RotateBy(90, 1)
```

```
LEFT = ac.RotateBy(-90, 1)

def move(x, y):
    dur = abs(x+y) / 100.0
    return ac.MoveBy((x, y), duration=dur)
```

With these constants and the auxiliary function, we can easily create a list of actions that will be chained to represent the complete list of steps required to follow the green path shown in the previous screenshot. For instance, this could be a hypothetical usage of these utilities to compose a chain of actions:

```
steps = [move(610, 0), LEFT, move(0, 160), LEFT, move(-415, 0),
         RIGHT, move(0, 160), RIGHT, move(420, 0)]
for step in steps:
    actions += step
sprite.do(actions)
```

This solution not only avoids the need to write all the steps one by one, but also makes our code more expressive and readable. Now let's encapsulate this logic in a class that will hold this data.

Domain-specific languages

This use of abstractions to represent high-level concepts is widely found in programming, and game development is not an exception. When this syntax reaches a whole domain of specialized features, the resulting language is called a **Domain-specific Language (DSL)**.

While this small domain only covers sprite movements and cannot be considered a DSL by itself, advanced game engines include specific scripting languages that are focused on game development.

The scenario class

Let's start the definition of the **scenario** module by creating an empty file called scenario.py and opening it with our favorite text editor. This module will contain the definition of the Scenario class, which groups the previously discussed information, such as the bunker's position, the chain of actions that the enemies will follow, and so on:

```
class Scenario(object):
    def __init__(self, tmx_map, turrets, bunker, enemy_start):
        self.tmx_map = tmx_map
        self.turret_slots = turrets
        self.bunker_position = bunker
        self.enemy_start = enemy_start
```

```
        self._actions = None

    def get_background(self):
        tmx_map = cocos.tiles.load('assets/tower_defense.tmx')
        bg = tmx_map[self.tmx_map]
        bg.set_view(0, 0, bg.px_width, bg.px_height)
        return bg
```

To retrieve the sequence of actions, we will use the @property decorator. It allows us to access to an attribute by invoking functions that will act as getters and setters:

```
    @property
    def actions(self):
        return self._actions

    @actions.setter
    def actions(self, actions):
        self._actions = ac.RotateBy(90, 0.5)
        for step in actions:
            self._actions += step
```

This decorator wraps the access to the internal _actions member. Given an instance of this class named scenario, the retrieval of the scenario.actions member would trigger the getter function, while an assignment to scenario.actions would trigger the setter function.

Now we can define a function that instantiates a scenario and set its members based on the disposition of our 'map0'. If we had designed more levels, we could have added more functions that create these new scenarios:

```
def get_scenario():
    turret_slots = [(192, 352), (320, 352), (448, 352),
                    (192, 192), (320, 192), (448, 192),
                    (96, 32), (224, 32), (352, 32), (480, 32)]
    bunker_position = (528, 430)
    enemy_start = (-80, 110)
    sc = Scenario('map0', turret_slots,
                  bunker_position, enemy_start)
    sc.actions = [move(610, 0), LEFT, move(0, 160),
                  LEFT, move(-415, 0), RIGHT,
                  move(0, 160), RIGHT, move(420, 0)]
    return sc
```

To use this module from another one, we will import it with this statement: from scenario import get_scenario. The next script that we will write is responsible for defining our game's main menu.

Transitions between scenes

In a previous section, you learned how to create a menu with cocos2d's built-in classes. The menu of our tower defense game will be very similar, since it follows the same steps. It will be implemented in a separate module, named `mainmenu`:

```
class MainMenu(cocos.menu.Menu):
    def __init__(self):
        super(MainMenu, self).__init__('Tower Defense')

        self.font_title['font_name'] = 'Oswald'
        self.font_item['font_name'] = 'Oswald'
        self.font_item_selected['font_name'] = 'Oswald'

        self.menu_anchor_y = 'center'
        self.menu_anchor_x = 'center'

        items = list()
        items.append(MenuItem('New Game', self.on_new_game))
        items.append(ToggleMenuItem('Show FPS: ', self.show_fps,
                                    director.show_FPS))
        items.append(MenuItem('Quit', pyglet.app.exit))
        self.create_menu(items, ac.ScaleTo(1.25, duration=0.25),
                         ac.ScaleTo(1.0, duration=0.25))
```

This menu displays three menu items:

- An option for starting a new game
- A toggle item for showing the FPS label
- A quit option

To start a new game, we will need the instance of the main scene. It will be returned by calling the `new_game` function of `mainscene.py`, which has not been developed yet. Besides, we will add a transition with the `FadeTRTransition` class from the `cocos.scenes.transitions` module.

A transition is a scene that performs a visual effect before setting the control of a new scene. It receives this scene as its first argument and some options, such as the transition duration in seconds:

```
from cocos.scenes.transitions import FadeTRTransition
from mainscene import new_game

game_scene = new_game()  # Instance of cocos.scene.Scene
transition = FadeTRTransition(game_scene, duration=2)
```

Now, to replace the current scene with the new one decorated with a transition, we call `director.push`. In this way, the `on_start_menu` method of our `MainMenu` class is implemented:

```
def on_new_game(self):
    director.push(FadeTRTransition(new_game(), duration=2))
```

The visual effect produced by this transition is that the current scene's tiles fade from the left-bottom corner to the top-right corner, as shown here:

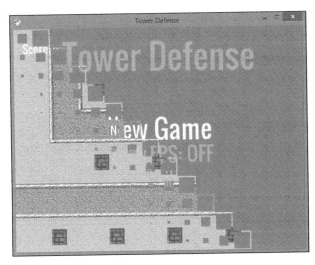

You can find the complete code of this module in the `mainmenu.py` script.

Game over cut scene

To create a cut scene when the game is over, we will need a simple layer and a text label. Since a scene is a `CocosNode`, we can apply actions to it. To hold this screen for a moment, it will perform a `Delay` action that lasts 3 seconds, and then it will trigger a `FadeTransition` to the main menu.

We will wrap these steps in a separate function, which will be part of another new module, named `gamelayer.py`:

```
def game_over():
    w, h = director.get_window_size()
    layer = cocos.layer.Layer()
    text = cocos.text.Label('Game Over', position=(w*0.5, h*0.5),
                    font_name='Oswald', font_size=72,
```

```
                              anchor_x='center',
                              anchor_y='center')
    layer.add(text)
    scene = cocos.scene.Scene(layer)
    new_scene = FadeTransition(mainmenu.new_menu())
    func = lambda: director.replace(new_scene)
    scene.do(ac.Delay(3) + ac.CallFunc(func))
    return scene
```

This function will be called from the game layer when the bunker's health points decrease to zero.

The tower defense actors

We will define several classes in the `actors.py` module to represent the game objects.

As with our previous game, we will include a base class, from which the rest of the actor classes will inherit:

```
import cocos.sprite
import cocos.euclid as eu
import cocos.collision_model as cm

class Actor(cocos.sprite.Sprite):
    def __init__(self, img, x, y):
        super(Actor, self).__init__(img, position=(x, y))
        self._cshape = cm.CircleShape(self.position,
                                        self.width * 0.5)

    @property
    def cshape(self):
        self._cshape.center = eu.Vector2(self.x, self.y)
        return self._cshape
```

In the `Actor` implementation in the previous chapter, when the sprite was displaced by calling the `move()` method, both `cshape` and `position` were updated at the same time. However, actions such as `MoveBy` only modify the sprite position, and the CShape center is not updated.

To solve this issue, we wrap the access to the CShape member through the `cshape` property. With this construct, when the `actor.cshape` value is read, the internal `_cshape` is updated by setting its center with the current sprite position.

This solution is possible because an object only needs a `cshape` member in order to be a valid entity for a `CollisionManager`, and a property is exposed in the same way as any other attribute that is directly accessed.

Now that our actor base class has been defined, we can start implementing the classes for the turrets and the enemy tanks.

Turrets and slots

Turrets are game objects that act autonomously; that is, there is no need to bind input events with their actions. The collision shape is not the sprite size but the firing range. Therefore, a collision between a turret and a tank means that the enemy is inside this range and can be considered a valid target:

```
class Turret(Actor):
    def __init__(self, x, y):
        super(Turret, self).__init__('turret.png', x, y)
        self.add(cocos.sprite.Sprite('range.png', opacity=50,
                                     scale=5))
        self.cshape.r = 125.0
        self.target = None
        self.period = 2.0
        self.reload = 0.0
        self.schedule(self._shoot)
```

The shooting logic is implemented by scheduling a function that increments the `reload` counter. When the sum of elapsed seconds reaches the `period` value, the counter is decreased and the turret creates a shoot sprite whose aim is at the current target:

```
    def _shoot(self, dt):
        if self.reload < self.period:
            self.reload += dt
        elif self.target is not None:
            self.reload -= self.period
            offset = eu.Vector2(self.target.x - self.x,
                                self.target.y - self.y)
            pos = self.cshape.center + offset.normalized() * 20
            self.parent.add(Shoot(pos, offset, self.target))
```

Apart from setting the target, a collision with the circular shape that represents the firing range also rotates the turret, giving the impression that it is aiming at the target.

To calculate the angle by which the sprite must rotate, we calculate the vector that runs from the turret to the target. With the `atan2` function from the `math` module, we calculate the angle between the π and -π radians formed by the positive x axis and this vector. Finally, we change the sign of the angle and convert it from radians to degrees:

```python
def collide(self, other):
    self.target = other
    if self.target is not None:
        x, y = other.x - self.x, other.y - self.y
        angle = -math.atan2(y, x)
        self.rotation = math.degrees(angle)
```

A `shoot` is not an actor, since it is not required to be able to collide. Through a sequence of actions, it will move from the turret to the tank's position and hit the `target` instance:

```python
class Shoot(cocos.sprite.Sprite):
    def __init__(self, pos, offset, target):
        super(Shoot, self).__init__('shoot.png', position=pos)
        self.do(ac.MoveBy(offset, 0.1) +
                ac.CallFunc(self.kill) +
                ac.CallFunc(target.hit))
```

Apart from `Turret` and `Shoot`, we will need a class to represent the slots in which the turrets can be placed. Since we will take advantage of the `CollisionManager` functionality to detect whether a `CShape` has been clicked on, this class only needs a `cshape` member:

```python
class TurretSlot(object):
    def __init__(self, pos, side):
        self.cshape = cm.AARectShape(eu.Vector2(*pos),
        side*0.5, side*0.5)
```

Instances of this class will be added to a different `CollisionManager` so that they do not conflict with the rest of the game objects.

Enemies

An enemy tank is an actor that follows the `scenario` path until it reaches the bunker at the end of the road. It is destroyed if the turret shots reduce its health points to zero.

The player increments their score each time a tank is destroyed, so apart from `health`, we will need a `score` attribute to indicate how many points the player earns:

```
class Enemy(Actor):
    def __init__(self, x, y, actions):
        super(Enemy, self).__init__('tank.png', x, y)
        self.health = 100
        self.score = 20
        self.destroyed = False
        self.do(actions)
```

Since we must differentiate between whether the tank has exploded because it has been defeated by the turrets or because it has reached the end point, we will use a `destroyed` flag. This flag will be set to `true` only if the tank is destroyed by a turret.

We also check the `CocosNode` flag called `is_running`, since it is set to `false` when the node is removed. Thus, we can prevent the tank from being removed when it has already been killed:

```
def hit(self):
    self.health -= 25
    self.do(Hit())
    if self.health <= 0 and self.is_running:
        self.destroyed = True
        self.explode()

def explode(self):
    self.parent.add(Explosion(self.position))
    self.kill()
```

Like the animations of our *Space Invaders* game, an explosion will be simulated with a fast sequence of sprites that lasts for 0.07 seconds. To avoid having too many sprite instances in our layer, the `kill()` method is called 1 second after the object instantiation:

```
raw = pyglet.image.load('explosion.png')
seq = pyglet.image.ImageGrid(raw, 1, 8)
explosion_img = Animation.from_image_sequence(seq, 0.07, False)

class Explosion(cocos.sprite.Sprite):
    def __init__(self, pos):
        super(Explosion, self).__init__(explosion_img, pos)
        self.do(ac.Delay(1) + ac.CallFunc(self.kill))
```

Bunker

You might remember the description of the gameplay. We need to keep the enemies away from a specific area. In our version, it is represented by a bunker that is placed at the end of the road.

The bunker instance only needs to process the enemy collisions and decrease its health points. The initial number of health points is 100, and each collision subtracts 10 points from this total:

```python
class Bunker(Actor):
    def __init__(self, x, y):
        super(Bunker, self).__init__('bunker.png', x, y)
        self.hp = 100
    def collide(self, other):
        if isinstance(other, Enemy):
            self.hp -= 10
            other.explode()
            if self.hp <= 0 and self.is_running:
                self.kill()
```

As we did with the `Tank` class, we check whether the `CocosNode` flag `is_running` is set to `true` to avoid calling `kill()` when the bunker has already been removed.

Game scene

The game layer contains several attributes for holding the reference to the HUD layer, the scenario, and the game information, such as the score or the number of points that can be spent to build new turrets.

These classes are added to the `gamelayer` module, which has contained only the game over transition so far:

```python
class GameLayer(cocos.layer.Layer):
    def __init__(self, hud, scenario):
        super(GameLayer, self).__init__()
        self.hud = hud
        self.scenario = scenario
        self.score = self._score = 0
        self.points = self._points = 40
        self.turrets = []

        w, h = director.get_window_size()
        cell_size = 32
```

```
self.coll_man = cm.CollisionManagerGrid(0, w, 0, h,
                                        cell_size,
                                        cell_size)
self.coll_man_slots = cm.CollisionManagerGrid(0, w, 0, h,
                                              cell_size,
                                              cell_size)
for slot in scenario.turret_slots:
    self.coll_man_slots.add(actors.TurretSlot(slot,
                                              cell_size))


self.bunker = actors.Bunker(*scenario.bunker_position)
self.add(self.bunker)
self.schedule(self.game_loop)
```

Another difference from our previous cocos2d game is the usage of two collision managers: `coll_man` for the game actors and `coll_man_slots` for the turret slots. While the first one is updated during each iteration of the game loop, the second one contains static shapes that do not conflict with the actors' collisions. As a result, we avoid unnecessary additions and removals from the turret slot shapes; thus, improving the collision checking performance.

Both `points` and `score` are properties that, apart from accessing the `_points` and `_score` internal attributes, update the HUD with the new numeric value. Here, we will show the `points` property, but `score` has a similar implementation:

```
@property
def points(self):
    return self._points


@points.setter
def points(self, val):
    self._points = val
    self.hud.update_points(val)
```

The game loop is quite simple since the logic of the game is mainly implemented with actions:

```
def game_loop(self, _):
    self.coll_man.clear()
    for obj in self.get_children():
        if isinstance(obj, actors.Enemy):
            self.coll_man.add(obj)


    for turret in self.turrets:
```

```
        obj = next(self.coll_man.iter_colliding(turret), None)
        turret.collide(obj)
    for obj in self.coll_man.iter_colliding(self.bunker):
        self.bunker.collide(obj)

    if random.random() < 0.005:
        self.create_enemy()
```

These are the statements performed for each frame:

- It updates the collision manager with the positions of the enemy tanks.

- For each turret, we check whether there is any enemy within the firing range. If so, we call the `collide()` method of the `Turret` class.

- We also check whether a collision with the bunker has occurred. Since the only entities managed by `self.coll_man` are the enemy tanks, we do not have to worry about verifying that the other object is a tank and not a turret.

- Enemies are randomly spawned with a given probability. We left a static value, but it could have been calculated depending on the number of enemies defeated so that the game becomes increasingly more difficult.

The `create_enemy()` method places a new tank at the initial position. To prevent them from always spawning at the same coordinates, we will apply a random offset of +/- 10 pixels in both the x and y components:

```
def create_enemy(self):
    enemy_start = self.scenario.enemy_start
    x = enemy_start[0] + random.uniform(-10, 10)
    y = enemy_start[1] + random.uniform(-10, 10)
    self.add(actors.Enemy(x, y, self.scenario.actions))
```

The layer will process user input as usual, and we will register only one method to process mouse events. With the `objs_touching_point()` method, we will know whether any slot has been clicked on. If the player has enough points, a new turret instance is placed at the center of the slot's position:

```
is_event_handler = True

def on_mouse_press(self, x, y, buttons, mod):
    slots = self.coll_man_slots.objs_touching_point(x, y)
    if len(slots) and self.points >= 20:
        self.points -= 20
        slot = next(iter(slots))
        turret = actors.Turret(*slot.cshape.center)
```

```
        self.turrets.append(turret)
        self.add(turret)
```

Finally, we override the `remove()` method to detect which type of object has been removed:

```
def remove(self, obj):
    if obj is self.bunker:
        director.replace(SplitColsTransition(game_over()))
    elif isinstance(obj, actors.Enemy) and obj.destroyed:
        self.score += obj.score
        self.points += 5
    super(GameLayer, self).remove(obj)
```

If the node is the bunker, it means that the player has lost the game, and the director replaces the current scene with the **Game Over** cut scene. If the node is an enemy tank, the score and the points are updated before actually removing the object.

The HUD class

This layer is responsible for displaying the game information, a functionality similar to the HUD we built in our previous game:

```
class HUD(cocos.layer.Layer):
    def __init__(self):
        super(HUD, self).__init__()
        w, h = director.get_window_size()
        self.score_text = self._create_text(60, h-40)
        self.score_points = self._create_text(w-60, h-40)

    def _create_text(self, x, y):
        text = cocos.text.Label(font_size=18, font_name='Oswald',
                                anchor_x='center', anchor_y='center')
        text.position = (x, y)
        self.add(text)
        return text

    def update_score(self, score):
        self.score_text.element.text = 'Score: %s' % score

    def update_points(self, points):
        self.score_points.element.text = 'Points: %s' % points
```

Assembling the scene

To conclude our `mainscene.py` module, we will define the `new_game()` function. This function is used by the main menu when a new game is started. It returns the scene with the tile map, the HUD layer, and the game layer initialized and displayed in the correct order:

```
def new_game():
    scenario = get_scenario()
    background = scenario.get_background()
    hud = HUD()
    game_layer = GameLayer(hud, scenario)
    return cocos.scene.Scene(background, game_layer, hud)
```

The game will be started with the conditional block that we saw in our previous games. Apart from initializing the director and running the scene, we will load the Oswald font and add the images to the `resource` path with the Pyglet API:

```
from cocos.director import director
import pyglet.font
import pyglet.resource

from mainmenu import new_menu

if __name__ == '__main__':
    pyglet.resource.path.append('assets')
    pyglet.resource.reindex()
    pyglet.font.add_file('assets/Oswald-Regular.ttf')

    director.init(caption='Tower Defense')
    director.run(new_menu())
```

This is saved in the `towerdefense.py` script. The following screenshot shows the final project layout:

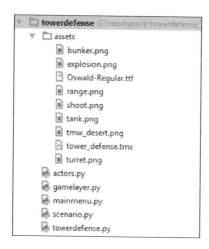

Summary

With this project, we saw how to include menus, transitions, and actions in our cocos2d applications. Our code is split into multiple modules, enhancing a better organization of our games.

This game can be the base for a more complex tower defense game. You can customize the number of points required to create a new turret, or change the probability of spawning enemies. As an exercise, try to create a new TMX map with Map Editor and define a custom scenario based on this background. *Your imagination is the limit!*

4
Steering Behaviors

Our previous cocos2d game was based on actions, so movements and rotations were predefined and the characters were not influenced by the current state of the game. However, a recurring problem in game development is how to recreate life-like animations, such as pursuing a target or avoiding moving obstacles.

Now, you will learn how to apply **steering behaviors**, a technique used to create seemingly intelligent movements for autonomous characters. The implementation of these strategies achieves the ability to navigate through the game world with improvised patterns.

Finally, we will put these strategies in practice with particle systems, a Cocos2d module that we have not worked with so far. Since we will use simple shapes, these particle systems will represent our characters, with the advantage of us not requiring external assets for our applications.

In this chapter, we will cover these topics:

- Basic concepts of steering behaviors
- Behaviors for individuals and groups
- Mixing these strategies
- How to render particle systems with cocos2d

NumPy installation

To use the particle system support of cocos2d, it is necessary to install NumPy, a Python package used to operate with large arrays and matrices in an efficient way. Since it contains several C modules, it might be difficult to install it on Windows systems because you might not have the appropriate compiler.

You can download the official binaries for Windows and Mac OS X from the NumPy site at `http://sourceforge.net/projects/numpy/files/NumPy/1.9.2/`.

Another option is to download the unofficial compiled binaries from Christoph Gohlke's website at `http://www.lfd.uci.edu/~gohlke/pythonlibs/#numpy`. Here, the packages are uploaded as .whl files. This is the extension of the wheel format and can be installed with `pip`:

```
$ pip install numpy-1.9.2+mkl-cp34-none-win32.whl
```

In both cases, remember to install the binaries for Python 3.4, since the versions for Python 2.7 and 3.3 are available for download as well.

You can check whether the installation was successful by running this command:

```
$ python -c "import numpy;print(numpy.version.version)"
1.9.2
```

Once NumPy is installed, you have all the requirements for supporting particle systems in cocos2d.

The ParticleSystem class

The base class for cocos2d particle systems is `ParticleSystem`, as defined in the `cocos.particle` module. The following table lists some of the most relevant class members. Note that the ones ending in _var indicate that random variance can be applied to the base value.

Class member	Description
Active	Indicates whether the particle system is spawning new particles or not.
Duration	The duration of the system in seconds. This value is -1 for infinite duration.
Gravity	Gravity of the particles.
angle, angle_var	The angular direction of the particles measured in degrees.
speed, speed_var	The speed of the particles.
tangential_accel, tangential_accel_val	Tangential acceleration.

Class member	Description
radial_accel, radial_accel_var	Radial acceleration.
size, size_var	The size of the particles.
life, life_var	The time in seconds for which each particle will live.
start_color, start_color_var	The start color of the particles.
end_color, end_color_val	The end color of the particles.
total_particles	The maximum number of particles.

You can create your own particle systems by extending this class and redefining the values of these class members.

Cocos2d includes another module, cocos.particles_systems, with some predefined ParticleSystem subclasses, each producing a different visual effect. The names of these classes are Fireworks, Spiral, Meteor, Sun, Fire, Galaxy, Flower, Explosion, and Smoke.

A quick demonstration

This code is a basic example that shows how to add a static ParticleSystem to our layer without processing any user input or actions:

```
import cocos
import cocos.particle_systems as ps

class MainLayer(cocos.layer.Layer):
    def __init__(self):
        super(MainLayer, self).__init__()
        particles = ps.Spiral()
        particles.position = (320, 240)
        self.add(particles)

if __name__ == '__main__':
    cocos.director.director.init(caption='Particles example')
    scene = cocos.scene.Scene(MainLayer())
    cocos.director.director.run(scene)
```

ParticleSystem inherits from CocosNode. Therefore, the instance has the usual members' position, rotation, and scale, as well as the do() and kill() methods.

Running this script shows the following predefined particle system:

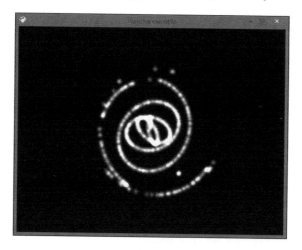

You can replace ps.Spiral() with other built-in particle systems, such as ps.Galaxy() or ps.Fireworks(). Many **Integrated Development Environments (IDE)**, such as PyCharm or PyDevm, offer code completion and will list all the names that are defined in a module after typing its name.

Implementing steering behaviors

The strategies that we will cover here have been taken from Craig Reynolds's paper *Steering Behaviors for Autonomous Characters*, written in 1999. It has become a well-known reference for implementing autonomous motion in an easy manner for non-playable characters.

You can check out the online version at http://www.red3d.com/cwr/steer/gdc99/. In this section, you will learn how to implement the following kinds of behavior:

- Seek and flee
- Arrival
- Pursuit and evade
- Wander
- Obstacle avoidance

Seek and flee

The **seek** behavior moves the character towards a specific position in the space. This behavior is based on the combination of two forces: the character's velocity and the steering force. This force is calculated as the difference between the desired velocity (the direction from the character to the target) and the character's current velocity.

Note that this is not a force in the strict physics definition; it is just another velocity vector. You can think of it as a *correction* of the character's velocity, and the resulting path will be a smooth curve that adjusts the velocity until it is aligned towards the target.

Flee is the inverse of seek, and it makes the character move away from the target. It means that the steering force pushes the character away from the target.

You can see both seek and flee represented graphically in the following diagram. The curved paths show the final direction once the forces are combined, the right one towards the target (seek), and the left one away from the target (flee).

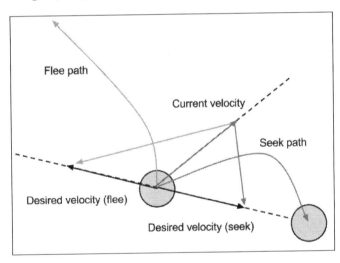

For our implementation, we need a class that represents the autonomous character with the following members:

- **velocity**: A two-dimensional vector representing the actor's velocity
- **speed**: The actor's speed, measured in the number of pixels per frame
- **max_force**: The maximum magnitude of the steering force
- **max_velocity**: The maximum magnitude of the velocity vector
- **target**: The position that the actor tries to reach

Besides, to put our particle systems into practice, we will extend `CocosNode` instead of `Sprite` and represent our actor with the `Sun` particle system:

```
import cocos
import cocos.euclid as eu
import cocos.particle_systems as ps

class Actor(cocos.cocosnode.CocosNode):
    def __init__(self, x, y):
        super(Actor, self).__init__()
        self.position = (x, y)
        self.velocity = eu.Vector2(0, 0)
        self.speed = 2
        self.max_force = 5
        self.max_velocity = 200
        self.target = None
        self.add(ps.Sun())
        self.schedule(self.update)
```

The `update()` method will compute the new position of the character for each frame, based on the current velocity and the target that it is seeking:

```
def update(self, dt):
    if self.target is None:
        return
    distance = self.target - eu.Vector2(self.x, self.y)
    steering = distance * self.speed - self.velocity
    steering = truncate(steering, self.max_force)
    self.velocity = truncate(self.velocity + steering,
                             self.max_velocity)
    self.position += self.velocity * dt
```

Step by step, we perform the following operations:

- Calculate the distance to the target.
- We scale this distance against the speed and subtract the current velocity. This gives us the steering force.
- Truncate this force with the maximum force.
- Sum the steering force with the current velocity and limit it to the maximum velocity that can be reached.
- Update the position with the velocity per frame.

This figure shows how these vectors are added to achieve the resulting path to the target:

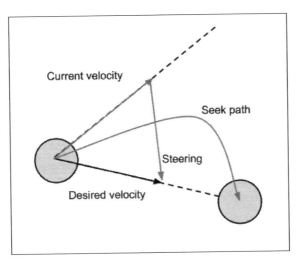

The `truncate()` function limits the magnitude of a vector, preventing the velocity from reaching a greater module than allowed:

```
def truncate(vector, m):
    magnitude = abs(vector)
    if magnitude > m:
        vector *= m / magnitude
    return vector
```

If the `vector` module is greater than the maximum value, the `vector` is normalized and scaled by this value.

The character's target will be the mouse pointer, and the target coordinates must be updated when the mouse is moved. To do so, we will define a custom layer that handles the mouse motion events and sets the actor's target:

```
class MainLayer(cocos.layer.Layer):
    is_event_handler = True

    def __init__(self):
        super(MainLayer, self).__init__()
        self.actor = Actor(320, 240)
```

```
        self.add(self.actor)

    def on_mouse_motion(self, x, y, dx, dy):
        self.actor.target = eu.Vector2(x, y)

if __name__ == '__main__':
    cocos.director.director.init(caption='Steering Behaviors')
    scene = cocos.scene.Scene(MainLayer())
    cocos.director.director.run(scene)
```

When you run this code, which is present in the `seek.py` script, the character will seek the mouse pointer when you move it over the window.

For the flee behavior, simply change the sign of the velocity when the position is updated:

```
    def update(self, dt):
        if self.target is None:
            return
        # ...
        self.position += self.velocity * dt * -1
```

This will make the character flee from the mouse pointer, and eventually leave the window if the mouse is closer to the center than the character. In the `seek_and_flee.py` script, you can find a combination of these implementations, where it is possible to switch them with the mouse click.

Arrival

You may notice that with the seek behavior, if the character's velocity is too high, it will pass through the target and come back smoothly.

The arrival behavior lowers the velocity once the character has reached a minimum distance close to the target, decreasing it gradually. This distance gives us the radius of the **slowing area**, a circle centered at the target position that causes the character's velocity to decrease.

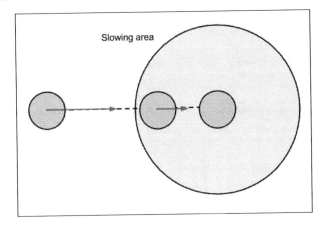

The implementation of this is quite similar to that of the seek behavior. We need to add the `slow_radius` member to indicate the radius of the slowing area:

```
class Actor(cocos.cocosnode.CocosNode):
    def __init__(self, x, y):
        super(Actor, self).__init__()
        self.position = (x, y)
        self.slow_radius = 200
        self.velocity = eu.Vector2(0, 0)
        # ...
```

With this attribute, we can modify our `update()` method so that the steering force is decreased linearly by the `ramp` factor. When the distance is greater than the slow radius, the `ramp` factor is at a minimum of `1.0`, so the steering force remains unmodified:

```
def update(self, dt):
    if self.target is None:
        return
    distance = self.target - eu.Vector2(self.x, self.y)
    ramp = min(abs(distance) / self.slow_radius, 1.0)
    steering = distance * self.speed * ramp - self.velocity
    steering = truncate(steering, self.max_force)
    self.velocity = truncate(self.velocity + steering,
                             self.max_velocity)
    self.position += self.velocity * dt
```

Note that when the distance approaches 0, the ramp factor equals 0 and the steering force becomes `-self.velocity`.

Check out the `arrival.py` file with the complete implementation of the behavior.

Pursuit and evade

The **pursuit** behavior is similar to seek, with the difference being that the character will move towards the position at which the target will be in the future based on the target's current velocity.

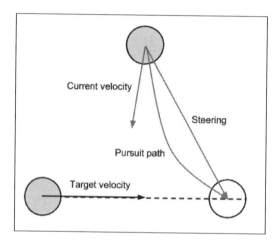

The **future position** is the sum of the target position plus the velocity vector multiplied by a unit of time. It gives the coordinates where the target will be placed within 1 second if it does not modify its velocity:

```
def update(self, dt):
    if self.target is None:
        return
    pos = self.target.position
    future_pos = pos + self.target.velocity * 1
    distance = future_pos - eu.Vector2(self.x, self.y)
    steering = distance * self.speed - self.velocity
    steering = truncate(steering, self.max_force)
    self.velocity = truncate(self.velocity + steering,
                             self.max_velocity)
    self.position += self.velocity * dt
```

If you want to set the future position as the coordinates where the target will be within 2 seconds, multiply the target's velocity by 2.

In this example, we will replace our mouse pointer target with a moving node. It will have a linear velocity, and our actor can use this velocity to calculate the future position:

```
class MainLayer(cocos.layer.Layer):
    def __init__(self):
        super(MainLayer, self).__init__()
        self.target = ps.Sun()
        self.target.position = (40, 40)
        self.target.start_color = ps.Color(0.2, 0.7, 0.7, 1.0)
        self.target.velocity = eu.Vector2(50, 0)
        self.add(self.target)
        self.actor = Actor(320, 240)
        self.actor.target = self.target
        self.add(self.actor)
        self.schedule(self.update)

    def update(self, dt):
        self.target.position += self.target.velocity * dt
```

On the other hand, for the evade behavior, we need to change only the last statement of the `update()` method to `self.position += self.velocity * dt * -1`, exactly as we did for the flee behavior.

The code of this behavior is included in the `pursuit.py` script.

Wander

The **wander** steering simulates a random walk without any specific target. It produces a casual movement without sharp turns or predictable paths.

It can be implemented with a seek behavior with targets calculated randomly. However, a more organic solution is to generate a random steering force towards a point on a circumference placed ahead of the character.

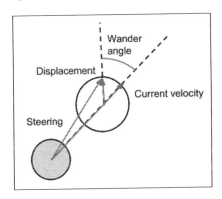

This force is calculated per frame, giving small random displacements that produce the visual effect of the character wandering around. This behavior can be parameterized with the following values:

- **wander_angle**: The current angle of displacement, to which the small variations will be added
- **circle_distance**: The distance of the character's position from the wander circle's center
- **circle_radius**: The radius of the wander circle
- **angle_change**: The factor by which the random value will be multiplied to produce a change in the wander angle

Now that we have seen how these forces are calculated, we can implement our wander behavior.

First of all, we will add these attributes to our `Actor` class:

```
import math
import random

class Actor(cocos.cocosnode.CocosNode):
    def __init__(self, x, y):
        super(Actor, self).__init__()
        self.position = (x, y)
        self.velocity = eu.Vector2(0, 0)
        self.wander_angle = 0
        self.circle_distance = 50
        self.circle_radius = 10
        self.angle_change = math.pi / 4
        self.max_velocity = 50
        self.add(ps.Sun())
        self.schedule(self.update)
```

With these members, we can modify our `update()` method:

```
    def update(self, dt):
        circle_center = self.velocity.normalized() * \
                        self.circle_distance
        dx = math.cos(self.wander_angle)
        dy = math.sin(self.wander_angle)
        displacement = eu.Vector2(dx, dy) * self.circle_radius
        self.wander_angle += (random.random() - 0.5) * \
                             self.angle_change
        self.velocity += circle_center + displacement
```

```
self.velocity = truncate(self.velocity,
                         self.max_velocity)
self.position += self.velocity * dt
self.position = (self.x % 640, self.y % 480)
```

These new statements perform the following operations:

- The circle's center is placed at the given distance ahead of the current character's velocity.
- We calculate the displacement with `wander_angle`, and it is scaled as per the radius of the circle.
- Given a random value between 0.0 and 1.0, we subtract 0.5 so that the value is between -0.5 and 0.5, thus preventing the angle from always changing by a positive value. We multiply this value by `angle_change` and add it to the `wander_angle` member.

You may notice another statement after the position is updated with the velocity. This last statement of the method is used to relocate the character, since it is very likely that the character will leave the screen due to the randomness of its movement.

Feel free to tweak the `circle_distance`, `circle_radius`, and `angle_change` values, and observe the differences that they cause to the player's movement.

Our main layer is simplified since it only needs to add the actor:

```
class MainLayer(cocos.layer.Layer):
    def __init__(self):
        super(MainLayer, self).__init__()
        self.actor = Actor(320, 240)
        self.add(self.actor)
```

The `wander.py` script contains the complete implementation of this behavior.

Obstacle avoidance

So far, we have not placed any barrier in our world, so the character can freely move around without avoiding any area.

However, most games place some obstacles, and the characters cannot pass through them. The **obstacle avoidance** behavior generates a steering force that causes the character to try and dodge these blocking items. Note that this does not perform collision detections, so if the current speed is high and the steering force module is not enough to counteract the character's velocity, the character might overlap with the shape of the obstacle.

To detect the presence of obstacles ahead, the character will keep an imaginary vector along its forward axis, which represents the distance up to which it can see ahead. The closest obstacle that collides with this segment, if any, will be the threat to avoid.

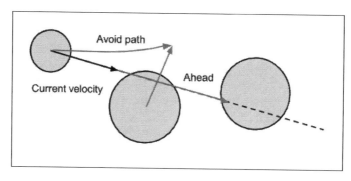

We will define an Obstacle class to represent the circular obstacles that we will use. Each of them can have a different radius, and we will keep track of all the created instances with a class member list:

```
class Obstacle(cocos.cocosnode.CocosNode):
    instances = []

    def __init__(self, x, y, r):
        super(Obstacle, self).__init__()
        self.position = (x, y)
        self.radius = r
        particles = ps.Sun()
        particles.size = r * 2
        particles.start_color = ps.Color(0.0, 0.7, 0.0, 1.0)
        self.add(particles)
        self.instances.append(self)
```

The Actor class will have two new attributes: **max_ahead**, the maximum distance at which the character can detect the presence of an obstacle, and **max_avoid_force**, the maximum force that can be applied to dodge an obstacle:

```
class Actor(cocos.cocosnode.CocosNode):
    def __init__(self, x, y):
        super(Actor, self).__init__()
        self.position = (x, y)
        self.velocity = eu.Vector2(0, 0)
        self.speed = 2
        self.max_velocity = 300
```

```
self.max_force = 10
self.target = None
self.max_ahead = 200
self.max_avoid_force = 300
self.add(ps.Sun())
self.schedule(self.update)
```

The `steering` force keeps seeking the target, with the difference that the `avoid` force is applied as well:

```
def update(self, dt):
    if self.target is None:
        return
    distance = self.target - eu.Vector2(self.x, self.y)
    steering = distance * self.speed - self.velocity
    steering += self.avoid_force()
    steering = truncate(steering, self.max_force)
    self.velocity = truncate(self.velocity + steering,
                             self.max_velocity)
    self.position += self.velocity * dt
```

The `avoid` force is calculated with the closest obstacle. To check whether the `ahead` vector intersects each obstacle, we will calculate the minimum distance from the circle's center to the vector. If this distance is lower than the circle's radius and it is the minimum distance, the obstacle is the closest one.

To find the distance between a vector and a point, we must project that point to the vector and see if it falls into its length. If it does, we calculate the distance between these two points, which is the distance between the vector and the point. Otherwise, it means that the point is behind or beyond the projection of the point on the vector.

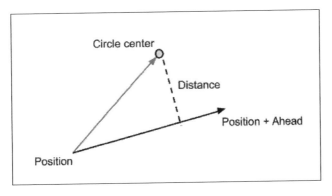

With these operations in mind, we can define the `avoid_force()` method:

```
def avoid_force(self):
    avoid = eu.Vector2(0, 0)
    ahead = self.velocity * self.max_ahead / self.max_velocity
    l = ahead.dot(ahead)
    if l == 0:
        return avoid
    closest, closest_dist = None, None
    for obj in Obstacle.instances:
        w = eu.Vector2(obj.x - self.x, obj.y - self.y)
        t = ahead.dot(w)
        if 0 < t < l:
            proj = self.position + ahead * t / l
            dist = abs(obj.position - proj)
            if dist < obj.radius and \
                (closest is None or dist < closest_dist):
                closest, closest_dist = obj.position, dist
    if closest is not None:
        avoid = self.position + ahead - closest
        avoid = avoid.normalized() * self.max_avoid_force
    return avoid
```

These are the steps performed by this method:

- We calculate the `ahead` vector and its squared length. If it is zero, it means that it does not see anything ahead and the avoidance force is `(0, 0)`.

- For each obstacle, we keep track of the distance between the `ahead` vector and the circle's center. If this distance is lower than its radius and it is the closest obstacle, we set it as the obstacle to avoid.

- Finally, if there is any obstacle selected, we scale the avoid force by the `max_avoid_force` factor.

We will add some obstacles to our `MainLayer`, and the actor will avoid them without any further reference to these new objects, since they are automatically added to the `Obstacle.instances` list:

```
class MainLayer(cocos.layer.Layer):
    is_event_handler = True

    def __init__(self):
        super(MainLayer, self).__init__()
```

```
        self.add(Obstacle(200, 200, 40))
        self.add(Obstacle(240, 350, 50))
        self.add(Obstacle(500, 300, 50))
        self.actor = Actor(320, 240)
        self.add(self.actor)

    def on_mouse_motion(self, x, y, dx, dy):
        self.actor.target = eu.Vector2(x, y)
```

You can check out the entire script in the `obstacles.py` file. Run it and move the mouse pointer above the screen to see how the character tries to avoid the obstacles represented by the green circles.

Gravitation game

To put into practice what you have learned about steering behaviors, we will build a basic game. The player's objective is to collect some pickup items that rotate around different planets placed in the world, while escaping from enemies. The enemies are non-playable characters that seek the playable character and avoid the planets.

We will represent the characters as particle systems, and the final version of the game will look like this:

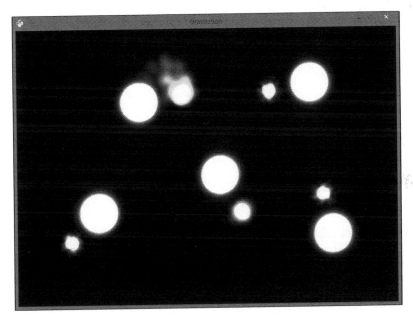

Basic game objects

As usual, we will define a base class that wraps the access to the `CircleShape` attribute with the updated center:

```
from cocos.cocosnode import CocosNode
from cocos.director import director
import cocos.collision_model as cm

class Actor(CocosNode):
    def __init__(self, x, y, r):
        super(Actor, self).__init__()
        self.position = (x, y)
        self._cshape = cm.CircleShape(self.position, r)

    @property
    def cshape(self):
        self._cshape.center = eu.Vector2(self.x, self.y)
        return self._cshape
```

Since some characters will rotate around the planets, we will define another class to update the position of the actor based on a rotational movement. This class will have a reference to the planet it is rotating around, the angular speed, and the current angle of rotation:

```
class MovingActor(Actor):
    def __init__(self, x, y, r):
        super(MovingActor, self).__init__(x, y, r)
        self._planet = None
        self._distance = 0
        self.angle = 0
        self.rotationSpeed = 0.6
        self.schedule(self.update)
```

Access to the `Planet` member will be implemented through a property, because when we set `planet`, we need to calculate the distance and the current angle:

```
    @property
    def planet(self):
        return self._planet

    @planet.setter
    def planet(self, val):
        if val is not None:
            dx, dy = self.x - val.x, self.y - val.y
            self.angle = -math.atan2(dy, dx)
            self._distance = abs(eu.Vector2(dx, dy))
        self._planet = val
```

The scheduled method increments the rotation angle with the elapsed time and updates the actor's position with the cosine and sine of this angle:

```
def update(self, dt):
    if self.planet is None:
        return
    dist = self._distance
    self.angle += self.rotationSpeed * dt
    self.angle %= math.pi * 2
    self.x = self.planet.x + dist * math.cos(self.angle)
    self.y = self.planet.y - dist * math.sin(self.angle)
```

Planets and pickups

Our `Planet` class will represent the static actors around which the pickups and the player rotate. We will keep track of all the instances, as we did with the `Obstacle` class previously:

```
class Planet(Actor):
    instances = []

    def __init__(self, x, y, r=50):
        super(Planet, self).__init__(x, y, r)
        particles = ps.Sun()
        particles.start_color = ps.Color(0.5, 0.5, 0.5, 1.0)
        particles.size = r * 2
        self.add(particles)
        self.instances.append(self)
```

Pickups will be moving actors, so we will inherit from `MovingActor`, which has implemented this functionality:

```
class PickupParticles(ps.Sun):
    size = 20
    start_color = ps.Color(0.7, 0.7, 0.2, 1.0)


class Pickup(MovingActor):
    def __init__(self, x, y, planet):
        super(Pickup, self).__init__(x, y, 10)
        self.planet = planet
        self.gravity_factor = 50
        self.particles = PickupParticles()
        self.add(self.particles)
```

Player and enemies

The player character revolves around the planets like the pickups do, but with the difference that it can switch from one planet to another when the spacebar is pressed.

This is the control that the player has over the actor, so we will need to add a linear speed to implement this kind of movement, which extends the logic offered by the MovingActor class:

```
class Player(MovingActor):
    def __init__(self, x, y, planet):
        super(Player, self).__init__(x, y, 16)
        self.planet = planet
        self.rotationSpeed = 1
        self.linearSpeed = 80
        self.direction = eu.Vector2(0, 0)
        self.particles = ps.Meteor()
        self.particles.size = 50
        self.add(self.particles)
```

Now the update() method performs a linear movement when the player is not revolving around any planet:

```
def update(self, dt):
    if self.planet is not None:
        super(Player, self).update(dt)
        gx = 20 * math.cos(self.angle)
        gy = 20 * math.sin(self.angle)
        self.particles.gravity = eu.Point2(gx, -gy)
    else:
        self.position += self.direction * dt
```

Finally, we need to implement the method that triggers the switch from one planet to another. It calculates the direction vector depending on the current angle of rotation with respect to the planet:

```
def switch(self):
    new_dir = eu.Vector2(self.y - self.planet.y,
                         self.planet.x - self.x)
    self.direction = new_dir.normalized() * self.linearSpeed
    self.planet = None
    self.particles.gravity = eu.Point2(-self.direction.x,
                                       -self.direction.y)
```

You may notice that the gravity of the particles is updated with the player's movement. This gives visual feedback of the current direction of the character and the position it is pointing to.

The implementation of the `Enemy` class is almost the same as the one we saw with the obstacle avoidance behavior. The main differences are that this class uses the `Planet.instances`: list and the radius of the obstacles is retrieved from the `cshape` member of each planet:

```
def avoid_force(self):
    # ...
    closest, closest_dist = None, None
    for obj in Planet.instances:
        w = eu.Vector2(obj.x - self.x, obj.y - self.y)
        t = ahead.dot(w)
        if 0 < t < l:
            proj = self.position + ahead * t / l
            dist = abs(obj.position - proj)
            if dist < obj.cshape.r and \
                (closest is None or dist < closest_dist):
                closest, closest_dist = obj.position, dist
    if closest is not None:
        avoid = self.position + ahead - closest
        avoid = avoid.normalized() * self.max_avoid_force
    return avoid
```

Explosions

There are some collisions that can trigger a game event. For instance, when an item is picked up by the player, it must be removed, or when the playable character hits an enemy or a planet, it is destroyed and spawns again in its original position.

One way to enhance these situations is through explosions; they give visual feedback to the player. We will implement them with a custom particle system:

```
class ActorExplosion(ps.ParticleSystem):
    total_particles = 400
    duration = 0.1
    gravity = eu.Point2(0, 0)
    angle = 90.0
    angle_var = 360.0
    speed = 40.0
    speed_var = 20.0
```

```
life = 3.0
life_var = 1.5
emission_rate = total_particles / duration
start_color_var = ps.Color(0.0, 0.0, 0.0, 0.2)
end_color = ps.Color(0.0, 0.0, 0.0, 1.0)
end_color_var = ps.Color(0.0, 0.0, 0.0, 0.0)
size = 15.0
size_var = 10.0
blend_additive = True

def __init__(self, pos, particles):
    super(ActorExplosion, self).__init__()
    self.position = pos
    self.start_color = particles.start_color
```

The game layer

All the game objects that we have developed will be added to the main game layer.
As usual, it will contain a collision manager that covers the entire window:

```
class GameLayer(cocos.layer.Layer):
    def __init__(self):
        super(GameLayer, self).__init__()
        x, y = director.get_window_size()
        cell_size = 32
        self.coll_man = cm.CollisionManagerGrid(0, x, \
                            0, y, cell_size, cell_size)
        self.planet_area = 400
        planet1 = self.add_planet(450, 280)
        planet2 = self.add_planet(180, 200)
        planet3 = self.add_planet(270, 440)
        planet4 = self.add_planet(650, 480)
        planet5 = self.add_planet(700, 150)
        self.add_pickup(250, 250, planet2)
        self.add_pickup(740, 480, planet4)
        self.add_pickup(700, 60, planet5)
        self.player = Player(300, 350, planet3)
        self.add(self.player)
        self.add(Enemy(600, 100, self.player))
        self.schedule(self.game_loop)
```

We also defined a couple of helper methods to avoid repeating the same code during initialization:

```
def add_pickup(self, x, y, target):
    pickup = Pickup(x, y, target)
    self.add(pickup)

def add_planet(self, x, y):
    planet = Planet(x, y)
    self.add(planet)
    return planet
```

Once the scenario is set up with the positions of the characters, and what actors are rotating around each planet, we can implement the game loop:

```
def game_loop(self, _):
    self.coll_man.clear()
    for node in self.get_children():
        if isinstance(node, Actor):
            self.coll_man.add(node)
    if self.player.is_running:
        self.process_player_collisions()

def process_player_collisions(self):
    player = self.player
    for obj in self.coll_man.iter_colliding(player):
        if isinstance(obj, Pickup):
            self.add(ActorExplosion(obj.position,
                                    obj.particles))
            obj.kill()
        else:
            self.add(ActorExplosion(player.position,
                                    player.particles))
            player.kill()
```

The layer must process the input events, specifically the spacebar press that triggers when the player's character stops rotating around a planet and leaves the orbit in a perpendicular direction.

When the spacebar is pressed again, the collision manager calculates what the closest planet is within a specific distance—which we set up in the __init__ method—and if there is any, it is set as the planet around which the target must rotate:

```
is_event_handler = True

def on_key_press(self, k, _):
```

```
        if k != key.SPACE:
            return
        if self.player.planet is None:
            self.player.planet = self.find_closest_planet()
        else:
            self.player.switch()

    def find_closest_planet(self):
        ranked = self.coll_man.ranked_objs_near(self.player,
                                        self.planet_area)
        planet = next(filter(lambda x: isinstance(x[0], Planet),
                            ranked))
        return planet[0] if planet is not None else None
```

Finally, do not forget to add the conditional block to run the script as the main
module. Here, we set the window's width and height:

```
if __name__ == '__main__':
    director.init(width=850, height=600, caption='Gravitation')
    director.run(cocos.scene.Scene(GameLayer()))
```

You can check out the complete game in the gravitation.py script. The game does
not require any extra assets, since all the rendered elements are based on the cocos2d
particle systems.

Summary

In this chapter, you learned several kinds of steering behavior that produce realistic
and autonomous navigations around your game world. These strategies might be
mixed, causing complex patterns and seemingly more *intelligent* actions.

Try to change the values of the constants used in each behavior to see how to achieve
different velocities and forces. Keep in mind the importance of generating smooth
movements instead of pronounced twists so that the experience is visually engaging.

Finally, we applied this knowledge in a basic game. Since it is a demonstration
of adding a non-playable character, the game can be complemented with all the
ingredients that we covered in the previous character (such as menus, transitions,
and so on).

In the next chapter, we will jump into 3D game development with OpenGL, a new
topic with more advanced features and details of a lower level.

5
Pygame and 3D

In our previous chapters, we developed our 2D games with Python modules that are built on top of a graphical user interface library, such as `Tkinter` and `Pyglet`. This allowed us to start coding our games without worrying about the lower-level details.

Now we will develop our first 3D game with Python, which will require an understanding of some basic principles of OpenGL, a popular multiplatform API for building 2D and 3D applications. You will learn how to integrate these programs with Pygame, a Python library commonly used to create sprite-based games.

In this chapter, we will cover the following topics:

- A steady approach to PyOpenGL and Pygame
- Initializing an OpenGL context
- Understanding the different modes that can be enabled with OpenGL
- How to render lights and simple shapes
- Integrating OpenGL with Pygame
- Drawing primitives and performance improvements

Installing packages

PyOpenGL is a package that offers Python bindings to OpenGL and related APIs, such as GLU and GLUT. It is available on the Python package Index, so you can easily install it via `pip`:

```
$ pip install PyOpenGL
```

However, we will need **freeglut** for our first examples, before we integrate OpenGL with Pygame. Freeglut is a third-party library that is not included if you install the package from PyPI.

On Windows, an alternative is to download and install the compiled binaries from `http://www.lfd.uci.edu/~gohlke/pythonlibs/#pyopengl`. Remember to install the version for Python 3.4.

Pygame is the other package that we will need in this chapter. It can be downloaded from the official website at `http://www.pygame.org/download.shtml`. You can install it from source if you want to; the compilation page contains the steps for building Pygame on different platforms.

Windows users can directly use the MSI for Python 3.2 or download *Unofficial Windows Binaries* from the Christoph Gohlke's website (`http://www.lfd.uci.edu/~gohlke/pythonlibs/`).

Macintosh users can find the instructions required to compile it from source on the Pygame website at `http://pygame.org/wiki/macintosh`.

Getting started with OpenGL

OpenGL is a broad topic in itself, and it is possible to find plenty of tutorials, books, and other resources, usually targeted at C or C++.

Since this chapter is not intended to be a comprehensive guide for this specification, we will take advantage of GLUT, which stands for **OpenGL Utility Toolkit**. It is widely used in small applications because of its simplicity and portability, and the bindings are implemented in PyOpenGL.

GLUT will help us perform some basic operations, such as creating windows and handling input events.

GLUT licensing

Unfortunately, GLUT is not in the public domain. The copyright is maintained by its author, Mark Kilgard, who wrote it for the sample programs included in *Red Book*, the official OpenGL programming guide.

This is the reason we are using `freeglut`, one of the open source alternatives that implement the GLUT API.

Initializing the window

The first lines of our script will be the `import` statements as well as the definition of our `App` class and its `__init__` method.

Apart from the OpenGL API and GLUT, we import the **OpenGL Utility Library (GLU)**. GLU is usually distributed with the basic OpenGL package, and we will use a couple of functions offered by this library in our example:

```python
import sys
import math

from OpenGL.GL import *
from OpenGL.GLU import *
from OpenGL.GLUT import *

class App(object):
    def __init__(self, width=800, height=600):
        self.title = b'OpenGL demo'
        self.width = width
        self.height = height
        self.angle = 0
        self.distance = 20
```

You may wonder what the b before the `'OpenGL demo'` string means. It represents a binary string, and it is one of the differences between Python 2 and 3. Therefore, if you find a GLUT program written in Python 2, remember that the string title of the window must be defined as a binary string in order to work with Python 3.

With these instance members, we can call our OpenGL initialization functions:

```python
def start(self):
    glutInit()
    glutInitDisplayMode(GLUT_DOUBLE | GLUT_DEPTH)
    glutInitWindowPosition(50, 50)
    glutInitWindowSize(self.width, self.height)
    glutCreateWindow(self.title)

    glEnable(GL_DEPTH_TEST)
    glEnable(GL_LIGHTING)
    glEnable(GL_LIGHT0)
```

Step by step, our `start` method performs the following operations:

- **glutInit()**: This initializes the GLUT library. While it is possible to pass parameters to this function, we will leave this call without any arguments.

- **glutInitDisplayMode()**: This sets the display mode of the top-level window that we will create. The mode is the bitwise OR of a few GLUT display mode masks. GLUT_DOUBLE is the mode for the double buffer, which creates separate front and back buffers. While one of these buffers is being displayed, the other one is being rendered. On the other hand, GLUT_DEPTH requests a depth buffer for the window. It stores the z coordinate of each generated pixel, and if the same pixel is rendered for a second time because two objects overlap, it determines which object is closer to the camera, that is, reproducing the depth perception.

- **glutInitWindowPosition()** and **glutInitWindowsSize()**: These set the initial position of the window and its size. According to our width and height instance members, it indicates to create a window of 800 x 600 pixels with an offset of 50 pixels in the x and y axes from the top-left corner of the screen.

- **glutCreateWindow()**: This creates the top-level window of our application. The argument passed to this function is a binary string for use as the window title.

- **glEnable()**: This is the function used to enable the GL capabilities. In our app, we call it with the following values:

  - GL_DEPTH_TEST: This performs depth comparisons and updates the depth buffer.

  - GL_LIGHTING: This enables lighting.

  - GL_LIGHT0: This enables Light0. PyOpenGL defines a specific number of light constants—from GL_LIGHT0 to GL_LIGHT8—but the particular implementation of OpenGL that you are running might allow more than this number.

Lighting and colors

When lighting is enabled, the colors are not determined by the glColor functions but by the combination of the lighting computation and the material colors set by glMaterial. To combine lighting with glColor, it is required that you enable GL_COLOR_MATERIAL first:

```
glEnable(GL_COLOR_MATERIAL)
# ...
glColor4f(r, g, b, a)
# Draw polygons
```

Once we have initialized GLUT and enabled the GL capabilities, we complete our start() method by specifying the clear color, setting the perspective, and starting the main loop:

```python
def start(self):
    # ...
    glClearColor(.1, .1, .1, 1)
    glMatrixMode(GL_PROJECTION)
    aspect = self.width / self.height
    gluPerspective(40., aspect, 1., 40.)
    glMatrixMode(GL_MODELVIEW)

    glutDisplayFunc(self.display)
    glutSpecialFunc(self.keyboard)
    glutMainLoop()

def keyboard(self, key, x, y):
    pass
```

These statements perform the following operations:

- **glClearColor()**: This defines the clear values for the color buffer; that is, each pixel will have this value if no other color is rendered in this pixel.

- **glMatrixMode()**: This sets the matrix stack mode for matrix operations, in this case to the projection matrix stack. OpenGL concatenates matrix operations for hierarchical modes, making it easy to compose the transformation of a child object relative to its parent. With GL_PROJECTION, we set the matrix mode for the projection matrix stack.

- **gluPerspective()**: The previous statement sets the projection matrix stack as the current stack. With this function, we can generate the perspective projection matrix. The parameters that generate this matrix are as follows:

  - fovy: The view angle in degrees in the y direction.
  - aspect: This is the aspect ratio of the field of view. It is the ratio of the viewport width to the viewport height.
  - zNear: The distance from the viewer to the **Near plane**.

○   `zFar`: The distance from the viewer to the **Far plane**.

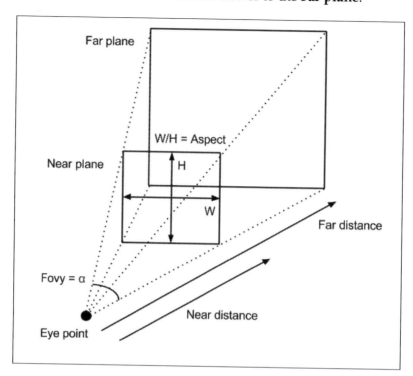

With `glMatrixMode(GL_MODELVIEW)`, we set the `modelview` matrix stack, which is the initial value, as the current matrix mode.

The last three GLUT calls do the following:

- **glutDisplayFunc()**: This receives the function that will be invoked to display the window.
- **glutSpecialFunc()**: This sets the keyboard callback for the current window. Note that this callback will be triggered only when the keys represented by the `GLUT_KEY_*` constants are pressed.
- **glutMainLoop()**: This starts the main loop of the application.

With the OpenGL context initialized, we are able to call the OpenGL functions that will render our scene.

The OpenGL and GLUT reference

As you may have already noticed, the OpenGL and GLUT specifications define a large number of functions. You can find the bindings of these APIs implemented by PyOpenGL on the official website at `http://pyopengl.sourceforge.net/documentation/manual-3.0/index.html`.

Drawing shapes

Our `display()` function performs the very common tasks of a main game loop.

It first clears the screen, then sets up a viewing transformation (we will see what this means after the snippet), and finally renders the light and draws the game objects:

```
def display(self):
    x = math.sin(self.angle) * self.distance
    z = math.cos(self.angle) * self.distance

    glClear(GL_COLOR_BUFFER_BIT | GL_DEPTH_BUFFER_BIT)
    glLoadIdentity()
    gluLookAt(x, 0, z,
              0, 0, 0,
              0, 1, 0)

    glLightfv(GL_LIGHT0, GL_POSITION, [15, 5, 15, 1])
    glLightfv(GL_LIGHT0, GL_DIFFUSE, [1., 1., 1., 1.])
    glLightfv(GL_LIGHT0, GL_CONSTANT_ATTENUATION, 0.1)
    glLightfv(GL_LIGHT0, GL_LINEAR_ATTENUATION, 0.05)

    glPushMatrix()
    glMaterialfv(GL_FRONT, GL_DIFFUSE, [1., 1., 1., 1.])
    glutSolidSphere(2, 40, 40)
    glPopMatrix()

    glPushMatrix()
    glTranslatef(4, 2, 0)
    glMaterialfv(GL_FRONT, GL_DIFFUSE, [1.,0.4,0.4,1.0])
    glutSolidSphere(1, 40, 40)
    glPopMatrix()

    glutSwapBuffers()
```

These are the operations that `display()` performs:

- **glClear()**: With the `GL_COLOR_BUFFER_BIT` and `GL_DEPTH_BUFFER_BIT` masks, this clears the color and depth buffers.

- **glLoadIdentity()**: This loads the identity matrix as the current matrix. The identity matrix is a 4 x 4 matrix with ones in the main diagonal and zeros everywhere else. This makes the stack matrix start over at the origin, which is useful if you have previously applied some matrix transformations.

- **gluLookAt()**: This creates a viewing matrix. The first three parameters are the x, y, and z coordinates of the eye point. The next three parameters are the x, y, and z coordinates of the reference point, that is, the position the camera is looking at. Finally, the last three parameters specify the direction of the up vector (usually, it is 0, 1, 0).

- **glLightfv()**: This sets the parameters of light source 0 (`GL_LIGHT0`). The following parameters are specified in our example:
  - `GL_POSITION`: This defines the position of the light
  - `GL_DIFFUSE`: This sets the RGBA intensity of the light
  - `GL_CONSTANT_ATTENUATION`: This specifies the constant attenuation factor
  - `GL_LINEAR_ATTENUATION`: This specifies the linear attenuation factor

Once the lighting attributes are set, we can start rendering basic shapes with GLUT. If we draw the objects first, lighting will not be applied correctly:

- **glPushMatrix()**: This pushes a new matrix into the current matrix stack, identical to the one below it. While we do this, we can apply transformations such as `glTranslate` and `glRotate`, to this matrix. We will render our first sphere at the origin, but the second one will be transformed with `glTranslate`.

- **glTranslate()**: This multiplies the current matrix by the translation matrix. In our example, the translation values for the second sphere are 4 for the x axis, and 2 for the y axis.

- **glMaterialfv()**: This sets the material parameters of the front face, as it is called with `GL_FONT`. With `GL_DIFFUSE`, we specify that we are setting the RGBA reflectance of the material.

- **glutSolidSphere()**: Through GLUT, this routine allows us to easily draw a solid sphere. It receives the sphere's radius as the first argument, and the number of slices and stacks into which the sphere will be subdivided. The greater these values are, the rounder the sphere will be.

- **glPopMatrix()**: This pops the current matrix from the stack. If we did not do this, each new object rendered would be a child of the previous one.

Finally, we switch the buffers with `glutSwapBuffers()`. If double buffering was not enabled, we should call the single buffer equivalent—`glFlush()`.

Running the demo

As usual, we check whether the module is the main script for starting the application:

```
if __name__ == '__main__':
    app = App()
    app.start()
```

If you run the complete application, the result will look like what is shown in the following screenshot:

Refactoring our OpenGL program

As you may have seen, this example uses enough OpenGL calls to grow out of control if we do not structure our code. That's why we are going to apply some object-oriented principles to achieve a better organization, without modifying the order of the calls or losing any functionality.

The first step will be to define a `Light` class. It will hold the attributes needed to render the light:

```
class Light(object):
    enabled = False
    colors = [(1.,1.,1.,1.), (1.,0.5,0.5,1.),
              (0.5,1.,0.5,1.), (0.5,0.5,1.,1.)]

    def __init__(self, light_id, position):
        self.light_id = light_id
        self.position = position
        self.current_color = 0
```

Besides, this modularization will help us implement a new functionality: changing the color of the light. We set the current color index to 0, and we will iterate over the different colors defined in `Light.colors` each time the `switch_color()` method is called.

The `render()` method respects the original implementation of lighting from our non-refactored version:

```
    def render(self):
        light_id = self.light_id
        color = Light.colors[self.current_color]
        glLightfv(light_id, GL_POSITION, self.position)
        glLightfv(light_id, GL_DIFFUSE, color)
        glLightfv(light_id, GL_CONSTANT_ATTENUATION, 0.1)
        glLightfv(light_id, GL_LINEAR_ATTENUATION, 0.05)

    def switch_color(self):
        self.current_color += 1
        self.current_color %= len(Light.colors)
```

Finally, we wrap the call to enable lighting with the `enable()` method and a `class` attribute:

```
    def enable(self):
        if not Light.enabled:
            glEnable(GL_LIGHTING)
            Light.enabled = True
        glEnable(self.light_id)
```

Another improvement is the creation of a `Sphere` class. This class will allow us to customize the radius, position, and color of each instance:

```
class Sphere(object):
    slices = 40
    stacks = 40

    def __init__(self, radius, position, color):
        self.radius = radius
        self.position = position
        self.color = color

    def render(self):
        glPushMatrix()
        glTranslatef(*self.position)
        glMaterialfv(GL_FRONT, GL_DIFFUSE, self.color)
        glutSolidSphere(self.radius, Sphere.slices, Sphere.stacks)
        glPopMatrix()
```

With these classes, we can adapt our `App` class and create the instances that we will render in the main loop:

```
class App(object):
    def __init__(self, width=800, height=600):
        # ...
        self.light = Light(GL_LIGHT0, (15, 5, 15, 1))
        self.sphere1 = Sphere(2, (0, 0, 0), (1, 1, 1, 1))
        self.sphere2 = Sphere(1, (4, 2, 0), (1, 0.4, 0.4, 1))
```

Remember that before rendering the `light` object, we need to enable OpenGL lighting through the `light.enable()` method:

```
    def start(self):
        # ...
        glEnable(GL_DEPTH_TEST)
        self.light.enable()
        # ...
```

Now the `display()` method becomes succinct and expressive, since the application delegates the OpenGL calls to the object instances:

```
    def display(self):
        x = math.sin(self.angle) * self.distance
        z = math.cos(self.angle) * self.distance
```

```
glClear(GL_COLOR_BUFFER_BIT | GL_DEPTH_BUFFER_BIT)
glLoadIdentity()
gluLookAt(x, 0, z,
          0, 0, 0,
          0, 1, 0)
self.light.render()
self.sphere1.render()
self.sphere2.render()
glutSwapBuffers()
```

To complete our first sample application, we will add input handling. It allows the player to rotate the camera around the spheres and move forward or away from the center of the scene.

Processing the user input

As we saw earlier, **glutSpecialFunc** takes a callback function that receives the pressed key as the first argument, and the x and y coordinates of the mouse when the key was pressed.

We will use the right and left arrow keys to move around the spheres, and the up and down arrow keys to approximate or move away from the spheres. Besides all of this, the color of the light will change if we press *F1*, and the application will be closed if the *Insert* key is pressed.

To do so, we will check the values of the key argument with the respective GLUT constants:

```
def keyboard(self, key, x, y):
    if key == GLUT_KEY_INSERT:
        sys.exit()
    if key == GLUT_KEY_UP:
        self.distance -= 0.1
    if key == GLUT_KEY_DOWN:
        self.distance += 0.1
    if key == GLUT_KEY_LEFT:
        self.angle -= 0.05
    if key == GLUT_KEY_RIGHT:
        self.angle += 0.05
    if key == GLUT_KEY_F1:
        self.light.switch_color()
    self.distance = max(10, min(self.distance, 20))
    self.angle %= math.pi * 2
    glutPostRedisplay()
```

Note that we trimmed the value of the `self.distance` member, so its value is always between 10 and 20, and `self.angle` is also always between 0 and 2π. To notify that the current window needs to be redisplayed, we call `glutPostRedisplay()`.

You can check out the `Chapter5_02.py` script, which contains this refactored version of our application.

When you run it, press the arrow keys to rotate around the spheres and *F1* to see how the lighting affects the spheres' materials.

Adding the Pygame library

With GLUT, we can write OpenGL programs quickly, primarily because it was aimed to provide routines that make learning OpenGL easier. However, the GLUT API was discontinued in 1998. Nonetheless, there are some popular substitutes in the Python ecosystem.

Pygame is one of these alternatives, and we will see that it can be seamlessly integrated with OpenGL, even simplifying the resulting code for the same program.

Pygame 101

Before we integrate Pygame into our OpenGL program, we will write a sample 2D application to get started with Pygame.

We will `import` Pygame and its locals module, which includes the constants that we will need in our application:

```
import sys
import pygame
from pygame.locals import *

class App(object):
    def __init__(self, width=400, height=300):
        self.title = 'Hello, Pygame!'
        self.fps = 100
        self.width = width
        self.height = height
        self.circle_pos = width/2, height/2
```

Pygame uses regular strings for the window title, so we will define the attribute without adding b. Another change is the number of **frames per second (FPS)**, which we will later find out how to control via Pygame's clock:

```
    def start(self):
        pygame.init()
        size = (self.width, self.height)
        screen = pygame.display.set_mode(size, DOUBLEBUF)
        pygame.display.set_caption(self.title)
        clock = pygame.time.Clock()
        while True:
            dt = clock.tick(self.fps)
            for event in pygame.event.get():
                if event.type == QUIT:
                    pygame.quit()
                    sys.exit()
            pressed = pygame.key.get_pressed()
            x, y = self.circle_pos
            if pressed[K_UP]: y -= 0.5 * dt
            if pressed[K_DOWN]: y += 0.5 * dt
            if pressed[K_LEFT]: x -= 0.5 * dt
            if pressed[K_RIGHT]: x += 0.5 * dt
```

```
        self.circle_pos = x, y
        screen.fill((0, 0, 0))
        pygame.draw.circle(screen, (0, 250, 100),
                          (int(x), int(y)), 30)
        pygame.display.flip()
```

We initialize the Pygame modules with `pygame.init()`, and then we create a screen with a given width and height. The DOUBLEBUF flag is passed so as to enable double buffering, which has the benefits we mentioned previously.

The main event loop is implemented with a while block, and with the `Clock` instance, we can control the frame rate and calculate the elapsed time between frames. This value will be multiplied by the speed of movement, so the circle will move at the same speed if the FPS value changes.

With `pygame.event.get()`, we retrieve the event queue, and if a QUIT event occurs, the window is closed and the application finishes its execution.

The `pygame.key.get_pressed()` returns a list with the pressed keys, and with the key constants, we can check whether the arrow keys are pressed. If so, the circle's position is updated and it is drawn on the new coordinates.

Finally, `pygame.display.flip()` updates the screen's surface.

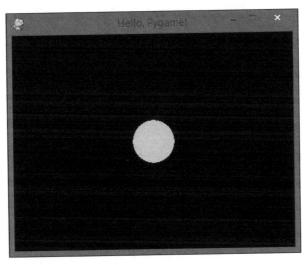

The `Chapter5_03.py` script contains the full code of this example.

The Pygame documentation

Since Pygame is divided into several modules, each one with various functions, classes, and constants, the official documentation is a useful reference.

We are using some functions from the key module; you can find further information about it at `https://www.pygame.org/docs/ref/key.html`. The same applies for the `display` and `time` modules.

Pygame integration

Let's see how it is possible to implement the same functionality with Pygame. The first step is to replace the `OpenGL.GLUT` import with the ones we used in our previous example:

```
import sys
import math

import pygame
from pygame.locals import *

from OpenGL.GL import *
from OpenGL.GLU import *
```

The `title` string is now a regular string, and the `FPS` attribute can be added as well:

```
class App(object):
    def __init__(self, width=800, height=600):
        self.title = 'OpenGL demo'
        self.fps = 60
        self.width = width
        self.height = height
        # ...
```

We remove the GLUT calls from our `start()` method, and they are replaced by the Pygame initialization. Apart from DOUBLEBUF, we will add the OPENGL flag to create an OpenGL context:

```
def start(self):
    pygame.init()
    pygame.display.set_mode((self.width, self.height),
```

```
                        OPENGL | DOUBLEBUF)
    pygame.display.set_caption(self.title)

    glEnable(GL_CULL_FACE)
    # ...
    glMatrixMode(GL_MODELVIEW)

    clock = pygame.time.Clock()
    while True:
        dt = clock.tick(self.fps)
        self.process_input(dt)
        self.display()
```

The new `process_input()` method updates the scene and the `instance` attributes by retrieving the events from the event queue and processing the pressed keys.

If a `QUIT` event occurs or the *Esc* key is pressed, the `Pygame` program is executed. Otherwise, the camera position is updated with the distance and angle of rotation, controlled by the arrow keys:

```
    def process_input(self, dt):
        for event in pygame.event.get():
            if event.type == QUIT:
                self.quit()
            if event.type == KEYDOWN:
                if event.key == K_ESCAPE:
                    self.quit()
                if event.key == K_F1:
                    self.light.switch_color()

        pressed = pygame.key.get_pressed()
        if pressed[K_UP]:
            self.distance -= 0.01 * dt
        if pressed[K_DOWN]:
            self.distance += 0.01 * dt
        if pressed[K_LEFT]:
            self.angle -= 0.005 * dt
        if pressed[K_RIGHT]:
            self.angle += 0.005 * dt

        self.distance = max(10, min(self.distance, 20))
        self.angle %= math.pi * 2
```

The `glutSwapBuffers()` is replaced by `pygame.display.flip()`, and the new `quit()` method quits Pygame and exits Python gracefully:

```
def display(self):
    # ...
    self.light.render()
    self.sphere1.render()
    self.sphere2.render()
    pygame.display.flip()

def quit(self):
    pygame.quit()
    sys.exit()
```

Another consequence of removing GLUT is that we cannot use `glutSolidSphere` to render our spheres.

Fortunately, we can substitute it with the `gluSphere` GLU function. The only difference is that we need to create a `GLUquadratic` object first, and then call the function with this argument and the usual radius, number of slices, and number of stacks into which the sphere is divided:

```
class Sphere(object):
    slices = 40
    stacks = 40

    def __init__(self, radius, position, color):
        self.radius = radius
        self.position = position
        self.color = color
        self.quadratic = gluNewQuadric()

    def render(self):
        glPushMatrix()
        glTranslatef(*self.position)
        glMaterialfv(GL_FRONT, GL_DIFFUSE, self.color)
        gluSphere(self.quadratic, self.radius,
                  Sphere.slices, Sphere.stacks)
        glPopMatrix()
```

With these changes, the GLUT API is now completely replaced by Pygame. Check out the `chapter5_04.py` script to see the complete implementation.

> **OpenGL and SDL**
> By including Pygame, we replace the GLUT API with **Simple DirectMedia Layer (SDL)**, which is the library that Pygame is built over. Like `freeglut`, it is another cross-platform alternative to GLUT.

Drawing with OpenGL

Until now, we have always rendered our objects with a utility routine, but most OpenGL applications require the use of some drawing primitives.

The Cube class

We will define a new class to render cubes, and we will use the following representation to better understand the vertices' positions. From 0 to 7, the vertices are enumerated and represented in a 3D space.

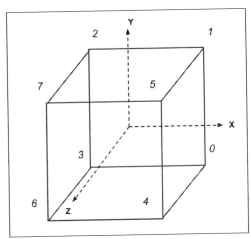

The sides of a cube can now be represented as tuples: the back face is `(0, 1, 2, 3)`, the right face is `(4, 5, 1, 0)`, and so on.

Note that we arrange the vertices in counterclockwise order. As we will learn later, this will help us enable an optimization called **face culling**, which consists of drawing only the visible faces of a polygon:

```
class Cube(object):
    sides = ((0,1,2,3), (3,2,7,6), (6,7,5,4),
             (4,5,1,0), (1,5,7,2), (4,0,3,6))
```

The __init__ method will store the values of the position and color, as well as the vertex coordinates with respect to the center position of the cube:

```
def __init__(self, position, size, color):
    self.position = position
    self.color = color
    x, y, z = map(lambda i: i/2, size)
    self.vertices = (
        (x,  -y, -z), (x,   y, -z),
        (-x,  y, -z), (-x, -y, -z),
        (x,  -y,  z), (x,   y,  z),
        (-x, -y,  z), (-x,  y,  z))
```

The render() method pushes a new matrix, transforms it according to its current position, and calls glVertex3fv() for each vertex of the six faces of cube.

The glVertex3fv takes a list of three float values that specify the vertex position. This function is executed between the glBegin() and glEnd() calls. They delimit the vertices that define a primitive. The GL_QUADS mode treats each group of four vertices as an independent quadrilateral.

The last statement pops the current matrix from the matrix stack:

```
def render(self):
    glPushMatrix()
    glTranslatef(*self.position)
    glBegin(GL_QUADS)
    glMaterialfv(GL_FRONT, GL_DIFFUSE, self.color)
    for side in Cube.sides:
        for v in side:
            glVertex3fv(self.vertices[v])
    glEnd()
    glPopMatrix()
```

Enabling face culling

Even though a cube has six faces, we can see a maximum of only three faces at once, and only two or one from certain angles. Therefore, if we discard the faces that are not going to be visible, we can avoid rendering at least 50 percent of the faces of our cubes.

By enabling face culling, OpenGL checks which faces are facing the viewer and discards the faces that are facing backwards. The only requirement is to draw the faces of the cube in the counterclockwise order of the vertices, which is the default front face in OpenGL. The implementation part is easy; we add the following line to our `glEnable` calls:

```
# ...
glEnable(GL_LIGHTING)
glEnable(GL_CULL_FACE)
# ...
```

In our next application, we will add some cubes and enable face culling to see this optimization in practice.

Basic collision detection game

With all of these ingredients, you are now able to write a simple game that detects simple collisions between shapes.

The scene consists of an infinite lane. Blocks appear randomly at the end of the lane and move towards the player, represented as the sphere in the following screenshot. He or she must avoid hitting the blocks by moving the sphere from right to left in the horizontal axis.

The game is over when the player's character collides with one of the blocks.

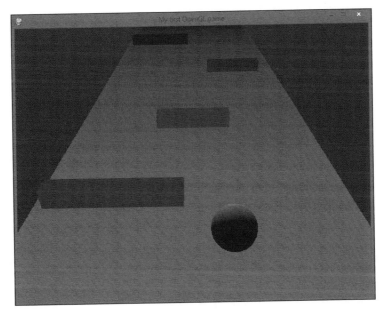

This gameplay is direct and uncomplicated, and it will allow us to develop a 3D game without worrying too much about more complicated physics calculations.

Since we are going to reuse the `Light`, `Cube`, and `Sphere` classes, we need to define a new class only to represent our game blocks:

```python
class Block(Cube):
    color = (0, 0, 1, 1)
    speed = 0.01

    def __init__(self, position, size):
        super().__init__(position, (size, 1, 1), Block.color)
        self.size = size

    def update(self, dt):
        x, y, z = self.position
        z += Block.speed * dt
        self.position = x, y, z
```

Its `update()` method simply moves the block towards the player by updating its z coordinate with uniform speed.

Our `App` class sets the initial values of the attributes that we will need during the execution of our game, and creates the `Light` and the game object instances as in our previous examples:

```python
class App(object):
    def __init__(self, width=800, height=600):
        # ...
        self.game_over = False
        self.random_dt = 0
        self.blocks = []
        self.light = Light(GL_LIGHT0, (0, 15, -25, 1))
        self.player = Sphere(1, position=(0, 0, 0),
                             color=(0, 1, 0, 1))
        self.ground = Cube(position=(0, -1, -20),
                           size=(16, 1, 60),
                           color=(1, 1, 1, 1))
```

The `start()` method has small variations, only adding `glEnable(GL_CULL_FACE)`, as we mentioned previously:

```python
def start(self):
    pygame.init()
```

```
# ...
glMatrixMode(GL_MODELVIEW)
glEnable(GL_CULL_FACE)
self.main_loop()
```

The `main_loop()` method is now a separate method and includes the random generation of blocks, collision detection, as well as the updating of the positions of the blocks:

```
def main_loop(self):
    clock = pygame.time.Clock()
    while True:
        for event in pygame.event.get():
            if event.type == QUIT:
                pygame.quit()
                sys.exit()
        if not self.game_over:
            self.display()
            dt = clock.tick(self.fps)
            for block in self.blocks:
                block.update(dt)
            self.clear_past_blocks()
            self.add_random_block(dt)
            self.check_collisions()
            self.process_input(dt)
```

We will implement collision detection by comparing the boundaries of the closest blocks with the extremes of the sphere. Since the sphere's width is smaller than the block size, if one of these extremes is between the right and left boundaries of a block, it will be considered as a collision:

```
def check_collisions(self):
    blocks = filter(lambda x: 0 < x.position[2] < 1,
                    self.blocks)
    x = self.player.position[0]
    r = self.player.radius
    for block in blocks:
        x1 = block.position[0]
        s = block.size / 2
        if x1-s < x-r < x1+s or x1-s < x+r < x1+s:
            self.game_over = True
            print("Game over!")
```

To prevent the spawning of too many blocks, we defined a counter called **random_dt**. It accumulates the elapsed time in milliseconds between frames, and it will try to spawn a new block only if the sum is greater than 800 milliseconds:

```
def add_random_block(self, dt):
    self.random_dt += dt
    if self.random_dt >= 800:
        r = random.random()
        if r < 0.1:
            self.random_dt = 0
            self.generate_block(r)

def generate_block(self, r):
    size = 7 if r < 0.03 else 5
    offset = random.choice([-4, 0, 4])
    self.blocks.append(Block((offset, 0, -40), size))
```

If the generated random number is lower than 0.1, a new block is added to the block list and the random_dt counter is reset to 0. In this way, the minimum elapsed time between two blocks can be 0.8 seconds, giving enough time to leave a tolerable distance from one block to another.

Another operation that the main loop performs is removing the blocks that are located behind the cameras' viewing area, avoiding the creation of too many Block instances:

```
def clear_past_blocks(self):
    blocks = filter(lambda x: x.position[2] > 5,
                    self.blocks)
    for block in blocks:
        self.blocks.remove(block)
        del block
```

The code for displaying the game objects stays as succinct as usual, thanks to the transfer of the drawing primitives to the respective render() methods:

```
def display(self):
    glClear(GL_COLOR_BUFFER_BIT | GL_DEPTH_BUFFER_BIT)
    glLoadIdentity()
    gluLookAt(0, 10, 10,
              0, 0, -5,
              0, 1, 0)
    self.light.render()
    for block in self.blocks:
        block.render()
```

```
self.player.render()
self.ground.render()
pygame.display.flip()
```

To finish our game, we will modify the input handling of our program. This change is straightforward, since we only need to update the x component of the character's position and trim it so that it cannot move out of the lane:

```
def process_input(self, dt):
    pressed = pygame.key.get_pressed()
    x, y, z = self.player.position
    if pressed[K_LEFT]:
        x -= 0.01 * dt
    if pressed[K_RIGHT]:
        x += 0.01 * dt
    x = max(min(x, 7), -7)
    self.player.position = (x, y, z)
```

In the chapter5_05.py script, you can find the full implementation of the game. Run it and feel free to modify and improve it! You can add pickup items and keep track of the score, or give the player a number of lives before the game is over.

Summary

In this chapter, you learned how it is possible to work with Python and OpenGL, and with basic knowledge about OpenGL APIs, we were able to develop a simple 3D game.

We saw two cross-platform alternatives for creating an OpenGL context: GLUT and Pygame. You can decide which one better suits your 3D games, depending on the trade-offs of each option. Keep this in mind: an advantage of using both is that you may adapt existing examples from one library to the other!

With these foundations of 3D covered, in the next chapter, we will see how to develop a 3D platformer based on these technologies.

6
PyPlatformer

So far, you have learned how to implement games in Python with different libraries, with the primary focus being on the practice of game development.

Now, we will introduce some theoretical concepts that will not only complement the practice, but will also help us develop games efficiently. This theory will aid us in understanding why games are conceptually designed the way they are.

In this chapter, we will cover these topics:

- Foundations of the game theory
- Object-oriented principles applied to game development
- How to implement a small 3D game framework
- Modularizing our functionality with reusable components
- Adding a physics engine to simulate rigid bodies' interactions
- Creating the building blocks of a platformer game

An introduction to game design

There are several academic definitions of what a game is; however, most of them share the key terms, such as rules, objectives, and players. Assuming that all games share these concepts, we may ask some interesting questions while analyzing a game: what is the game's main objective? What are the rules that the player must follow? Is it difficult to recognize the goal and the rules of the system?

Other definitions make references to concepts such as resource management and inefficiencies, because the decisions of the player are usually conditioned by the limitations of some useful tokens in the game.

The decisions we make when we create a game are deeply related with these concepts, and as we will see later, it is a good exercise to think about them even when we are starting with the development.

Level design

In order to successfully engage our players, our game needs to gradually add new challenges that preserve their interest. However, these ingredients should be introduced in a coherent order so that the player does not become confused because she or he does not know how to react to the game's output.

This means that the player is not only playing your game but also learning how to play it. This **learning curve** should be carefully considered in tutorials and the first level, because incorrect guidance can lead to frustration.

Platformer skills

In our platformer game, the first action that the player will learn is how to move their character, which is intuitively performed by pressing the arrow keys. Since there is not any threat nearby, the player can experiment moving around and can become familiar with the control keys.

Next, the player will face an obstacle, and she or he needs to learn how to jump over it to continue. There is no gap between the obstacle and the ground, so there is no risk of falling from the platform if the character's jump is too short, as shown in the following screenshot:

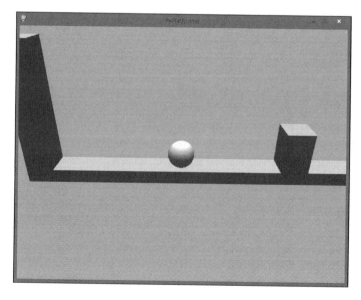

Once the first obstacle is cleared, the player faces a couple of platforms with gaps in between, as shown in the next screenshot. Now it is required to measure the jumping forces, or else the character will fall into the void.

If the character does not reach the platform and falls, it will respawn at the initial position. That's another lesson that the player will learn: move with care, or else you will have to start over again!

On the next platform, the player will encounter a new character. If the character collides with it, it will move back to the spawn position. Therefore, the player learns that these objects should be avoided and they must jump over it to advance.

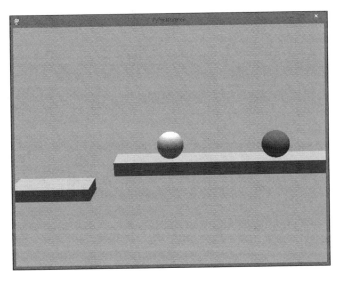

After this, the player can reach a platform on which there is a spinning box. It is placed in the middle of a narrow platform, so it is very easy to collide with, as shown in this screenshot:

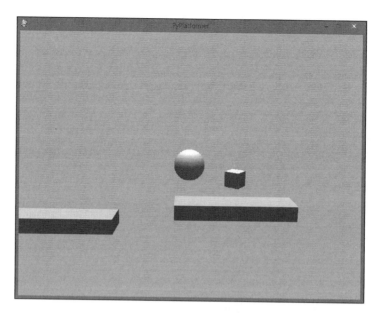

When this happens, the player's ammo is increased, so now the character is able to shoot by pressing the spacebar. On the next platform, the player can find another enemy to test their shooting ability. With the pickup, the player can shoot up to five times, so they can try out this ability several times before running out of ammo.

Now that we have analyzed the skills that our players will need to learn, we can move on to the architectural design of our game.

Component-based game engines

When we start developing a game from scratch, the first step may be to define a basic class with common attributes for all the game objects, such as its position coordinates, the color, the speed, and so on. This could be the basic `GameObject` or `Actor` class we declared in previous chapters.

Then you need to add other game objects with more concrete kinds of behavior, such as the character that will be controlled by the player, or the enemies that randomly shoot the playable character. If you represent these entities with separate classes, each one implements that functionality with a custom method in the corresponding class.

Consequently, every specialization of an existing entity might be translated into a new subclass. Suppose we want to add a special type of enemy that moves along a particular route, which we will call `PatrolEnemy`. In our class diagram shown here, this class will extend our `Enemy` class:

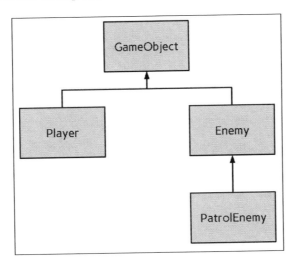

While this approach might work for small games, it becomes more difficult to scale the organization of the project when the inheritance hierarchy grows. Imagine that we want to add another type of enemy that shoots only when it is located within a certain distance from the player, and a third enemy that combines this new behavior with `PatrolEnemy`. This is illustrated in the following diagram:

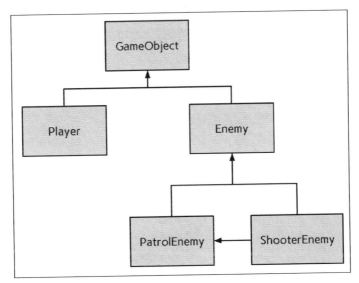

If some game objects follow the behavior of their ancestors and share the functionality with other entities, you may need to use multiple inheritance or define intermediate classes that would be unnecessary otherwise.

On the other hand, a component-based design follows the principle of favoring object composition over class inheritance. This means that the functionality is contained in other classes, instead of reusing it with a subclass.

Translated into our example, this architecture leaves us with the following diagram. Besides, as we will see later, a **component base** class is also added.

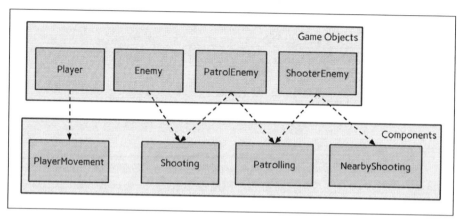

The classes under the **Game Objects** area are GameObject subclasses, but their behavior is determined by the composition of their **Components** subclasses.

In this way, we do not introduce multiple inheritance solutions and keep these pieces of functionality separated in small classes, with the advantage of being able to add or remove them dynamically.

In later sections, we will see how these components are also used to render objects in our OpenGL context, but now we will move on to the library that we will use to simulate physics in our game.

Introducing Pymunk

We will implement physics in our game with Pymunk, a 2D physics engine built on top of Chimpunk2D.

Even though we are using OpenGL for 2D graphics, our platformer game will recreate a two-dimensional space, so we will work on the plane in which the *z* axis equals *0*.

You can install Pymunk directly from `pip`:

```
$ pip install pymunk
```

The Chimpunk2D library is written in C, so you might need to compile it on your platform if the distribution does not ship with the precompiled library. On 32-bit Windows and 32-bit and 64-bit Linux versions, Pymunk will include the Chimpunk2D binaries.

For other platforms, or if you want to compile the library yourself, you can check out the installation guide and the steps for compiling Chimpunk2D at `http://pymunk.readthedocs.org/en/latest/installation.html`.

> **Don't reinvent the wheel!**
>
> Implementing a rigid body library is a laborious task, especially if you are developing a casual game from scratch — as we are doing in this chapter.
>
> Fortunately, the Pymunk API is simple and well-documented, so you can get started quickly and avoid losing time crafting a custom physics engine.

The main classes of the `pymunk` package are the following:

- **Space**: A two-dimensional space in which the physics simulation will occur. We will use a `Space` instance for the entire game, and we will update each frame through its `step()` method.

- **Body**: This represents the rigid body, the basic unit of simulation. It has a `position` member, which will also represent the position of the game object that contains the rigid body. The other members that we will cover are the `velocity` and `force` vectors.

- **Shape**: The base class for all shapes. We will limit ourselves to circle and box shapes, defined by the `Circle` and `Poly` classes respectively.

- **Arbiter**: This represents a collision pair between shapes and is used in collision callbacks. It also contains information about the contact points of the collision.

In the next section, we will rely on these classes and their attributes to hold information about game objects and their collisions.

Building a game framework

The `Component` and `GameObject` classes form the core of our game engine. The interface offered by the `Component` class is as easy as this:

```python
class Component(object):
    __slots__ = ['gameobject']

    def start(self):
        pass
    def update(self, dt):
        pass
    def stop(self):
        pass
    def on_collide(self, other, contacts):
        pass
```

These methods define the life cycle of our components:

- **start()**: This is called when the component is added to the game object instance. The component keeps a reference to the game object as `self.gameobject`.

- **update(dt)**: This is called for each frame, where the `dt` argument is the elapsed time in seconds since the previous frame.

- **on_collide(other, contacts)**: This is called when the component's game object collides with another rigid body. The `other` argument is the other game object of the collision pair, and `contacts` includes the contact points between the objects. This last argument is directly passed from the Pymunk API, and we will see later how to work with it.

- **stop()**: This is called when the component is removed from the game object instance.

These will be invoked from our `GameObject` class. As we mentioned earlier, a game object internally uses a rigid body to represent its position in the *x* and *y* axes and an extra variable for the *z* axis. By default, we will work in the *z=0* plane.

The `GameObject` class is defined as follows:

```python
import pymunk as pm

class GameObject(object):
    instances = []
```

```python
def __init__(self, x=0, y=0, z=0, scale=(1, 1, 1)):
    self._body = pm.Body()
    self._body.position = x, y
    self._shape = None
    self._ax = 0
    self._ay = 0
    self._z = z
    self.tag = ''
    self.scale = scale
    self.components = []
    GameObject.instances.append(self)
```

The two-dimensional position is complemented with an inner _z member, and the rotation is extended with the angle of rotation in the *x* and *y* axis with the _ax and _ay members, respectively. The velocity vector is directly retrieved from the rigid body:

```python
@property
def position(self):
    pos = self._body.position
    return pos.x, pos.y, self._z

@position.setter
def position(self, pos):
    self._body.position = pos[0], pos[1]
    self._z = pos[2]

@property
def rotation(self):
    return self._ax, self._ay, self._body.angle

@rotation.setter
def rotation(self, rot):
    self._ax = rot[0]
    self._ay = rot[1]
    self._body.angle = rot[2]

@property
def velocity(self):
    return self._body.velocity

@velocity.setter
def velocity(self, vel):
    self._body.velocity = vel
```

The game object's position can be modified by applying an impulse or a force vector to the underlying rigid body:

```
def move(self, x, y):
    self._body.apply_impulse((x, y))


def apply_force(self, x, y):
    self._body.apply_force((x, y))
```

The instance components can be manipulated—added, removed, and retrieved by type—in a flexible way with the following methods:

```
def add_components(self, *components):
    for component in components:
        self.add_component(component)


def add_component(self, component):
    self.components.append(component)
    component.gameobject = self
    component.start()


def get_component_by_type(self, cls):
    for component in self.components:
        if isinstance(component, cls):
            return component


def remove_component(self, component):
    component.stop()
    self.components.remove(component)
```

To display the game object, we pay special attention to the `Renderable` components. The interface of this `Component` subclass include a `render()` method, which is called in the display loop for each active game object.

The `update()` method directly delegates the execution to every attached component:

```
def render(self):
    for component in self.components:
        if isinstance(component, Renderable):
            component.render()


def update(self, dt):
    for component in self.components:
        component.update(dt)
```

Finally, when we remove a game object, we need to delete the shape of its rigid body from the Pymunk space; otherwise, the visual result will be such that the entities still keep colliding with an invisible object:

```
def remove(self):
    for component in self.components:
        self.remove_component(component)
    if self._shape is not None:
        Physics.remove(self._shape)
    GameObject.instances.remove(self)


def collide(self, other, contacts):
    for component in self.components:
        component.on_collide(other, contacts)
```

You can find the implementation of these two classes in the pyplatformer/ enginecomponents.py and pyplatformer/engine/__init__.py scripts.

> **Saving space consumption**
>
> By default, each object instance has an internal dictionary for attribute storage. The __slots__ class variable tells Python to allocate space only for each variable, saving space if the instance has few attributes.
>
> Since components are small classes, we added this optimization to avoid instantiating unnecessary dictionaries.

Now we will move on to the physics module, where the Input class and the shape components are defined.

Adding physics

This module is responsible for initializing the Pymunk Space. This happens at the beginning of the file, and the gravity and the collision handler are set to default values:

```
import pymunk

def coll_handler(_, arbiter):
    if len(arbiter.shapes) == 2:
        obj1 = arbiter.shapes[0].gameobject
        obj2 = arbiter.shapes[1].gameobject
        obj1.collide(obj2, arbiter.contacts)
        obj2.collide(obj1, arbiter.contacts)
    return True
```

```
space = pymunk.Space()
space.gravity = 0, -10
space.set_default_collision_handler(coll_handler)
```

The collision handler receives the space where the collision occurs as the first parameter and an **Arbiter** instance with the collision information. Here, we obtain the game object attached to the shape and trigger the `collide()` method.

The `Physics` class is similar to `Input`, since it contains a couple of class methods that wrap the basic functionality we are looking for:

```
class Physics(object):
    @classmethod
    def step(cls, dt):
        space.step(dt)
    @classmethod
    def remove(cls, body):
        space.remove(body)
```

The `Rigidbody` class is a base component that replaces the initial static body that every game object has with a non-static one. It also adds a reference to the game object from the shape, so it is possible to retrieve the game object from the Pymunk collision information:

```
class Rigidbody(Component):
    __slots__ = ['mass', 'is_static']

    def __init__(self, mass=1, is_static=True):
        self.mass = mass
        self.is_static = is_static

    def start(self):
        if not self.is_static:
            # Replace the static body
            pos = self.gameobject._body.position
            body = pymunk.Body(self.mass, 1666)
            body.position = pos
            self.gameobject._body = body

    def add_shape_to_space(self, shape):
        self.gameobject._shape = shape
        shape.gameobject = self.gameobject
        if self.is_static:
```

```
                space.add(shape)
        else:
                space.add(self.gameobject._body, shape)
```

 Note that static bodies are not added to the space; only their shapes are.

The `BoxCollider` and `SphereCollider` subclasses create the corresponding shape by calling the Pymunk API:

```
class BoxCollider(Rigidbody):
    __slots__ = ['size']

    def __init__(self, width, height, mass=1, is_static=True):
        super(BoxCollider, self).__init__(mass, is_static)
        self.size = width, height

    def start(self):
        super(BoxCollider, self).start()
        body = self.gameobject._body
        shape = pymunk.Poly.create_box(body, self.size)
        self.add_shape_to_space(shape)

class SphereCollider(Rigidbody):
    __slots__ = ['radius']

    def __init__(self, radius, mass=1, is_static=True):
        super(SphereCollider, self).__init__(mass, is_static)
        self.radius = radius

    def start(self):
        super(SphereCollider, self).start()
        body = self.gameobject._body
        shape = pymunk.Circle(body, self.radius)
        self.add_shape_to_space(shape)
```

Each implementation only differs in the information that is passed to build the shape, but you can easily add another rigid body component by following the same pattern.

Renderable components

The `components` module includes the definition of the `Renderable` class, which we mentioned earlier when we looked at how to display game objects.

It pushes a matrix to the current stack and performs some basic operations before delegating the rendering to the `_render()` method, saving us from repeating this boilerplate code:

```
class Renderable(Component):
    __slots__ = ['color']

    def __init__(self, color):
        self.color = color

    def render(self):
        pos = self.gameobject.position
        rot = self.gameobject.rotation
        scale = self.gameobject.scale
        glPushMatrix()
        glTranslatef(*pos)
        if rot != (0, 0, 0):
            glRotatef(rot[0], 1, 0, 0)
            glRotatef(rot[1], 0, 1, 0)
            glRotatef(rot[2], 0, 0, 1)
        if scale != (1, 1, 1):
            glScalef(*scale)
        if self.color is not None:
            glColor4f(*self.color)
        self._render()
        glPopMatrix()

    def _render(self):
        pass
```

The `Cube` and `Sphere` subclasses are an adaptation of the implementation we covered in *Chapter 5, PyGame and 3D,* and along with the `Light` class, they have been omitted for brevity.

The Camera component

You may remember how to set up the camera perspective with GLU, which was one of the first actions of the display loop in the previous chapter.

Now we will use a component to perform the same task, but it will differ from other components in the way in which it is called in the main loop. This happens because these matrix operations need to be the first ones of the OpenGL matrix stack if we want to set up the camera position correctly:

```python
class Camera(Component):
    instance = None

    def __init__(self, dy, dz):
        self.dy = dy
        self.dz = dz
        Camera.instance = self

    def render(self):
        pos = self.gameobject.position
        glLoadIdentity()
        gluLookAt(pos[0], self.dy, self.dz,
                  pos[0], pos[1], pos[2],
                  0, 1, 0)
```

The camera will look at the game object with which it is attached and the distance along the *y* and *z* axes are parameterized in its __init__ method.

This implementation takes the last camera that has been instantiated as the current one. In our game, we will only use a single camera component, and this can be considered a common scenario in basic games.

However, if you need to switch between multiple cameras, you can define a more complex component. As you may notice, these implementations are very clean and concise thanks to the assumption of these simplifications.

The InputManager module

To handle input events, we create a separate module that will wrap the processing of our pygame events. Since we will register keystrokes and the special QUIT event only, this class is quite uncomplicated:

```python
from collections import defaultdict
import pygame

class Input(object):
    quit_flag = False
    keys = defaultdict(bool)
    keys_down = defaultdict(bool)

    @classmethod
    def update(cls):
        cls.keys_down.clear()
        for event in pygame.event.get():
            if event.type == pygame.QUIT:
                cls.quit_flag = True
            if event.type == pygame.KEYUP:
                cls.keys[event.key] = False
            if event.type == pygame.KEYDOWN:
                cls.keys[event.key] = True
                cls.keys_down[event.key] = True

    @classmethod
    def get_key(cls, key):
        return cls.keys[key]

    @classmethod
    def get_key_down(cls, key):
        return cls.keys_down[key]
```

Note that with this interface, it is straightforward to get the pressed keys within any component, like this for instance:

```python
class HorizontalMovement(Component):
    def update(self, dt):
        direction = Input.get(K_RIGHT) - Input.get(K_RIGHT)
        self.gameobject.move(dt * direction * 5, 0)
```

We can subtract boolean values because bool is a subclass of int, and True corresponds to 1, while False corresponds to 0.

The Game class

The Game class is responsible for bootstrapping the application—setting the initial values of the window attributes, initializing the OpenGL context, and entering the game loop:

```python
class Game(object):
    def __init__(self, caption, width=800, height=600):
        self.caption = caption
        self.width = width
        self.height = height
        self.fps = 60

    def mainloop(self):
        self.setup()
        clock = pygame.time.Clock()
        while not Input.quit_flag:
            dt = clock.tick(self.fps)
            dt /= 1000
            Physics.step(dt)
            self.update(dt)
            self.render()
        pygame.quit()
        sys.exit()
```

Some of these initial operations have been extracted into the setup() method, so mainloop() stays clear and understandable:

```python
    def setup(self):
        pygame.init()
        pygame.display.set_mode((self.width, self.height),
                                pygame.OPENGL | pygame.DOUBLEBUF)
        pygame.display.set_caption(self.caption)
        glEnable(GL_LIGHTING)
        glEnable(GL_COLOR_MATERIAL)
        glColorMaterial(GL_FRONT_AND_BACK, GL_AMBIENT_AND_DIFFUSE)
        glEnable(GL_DEPTH_TEST)
        glClearColor(0.5, 0.7, 1, 1)
        glMatrixMode(GL_PROJECTION)
        aspect = self.width / self.height
        gluPerspective(45, aspect, 1, 100)
        glMatrixMode(GL_MODELVIEW)
```

The update() and render() calls delegate the execution to the game object instances, which in turn, will invoke their components' methods:

```
def update(self, dt):
    Input.update()
    for gameobject in GameObject.instances:
        gameobject.update(dt)

def render(self):
    glClear(GL_COLOR_BUFFER_BIT | GL_DEPTH_BUFFER_BIT)
    if Camera.instance is not None:
        Camera.instance.render()
    for gameobject in GameObject.instances:
        gameobject.render()
    pygame.display.flip()
```

The final arrangement of our **engine** package looks like this:

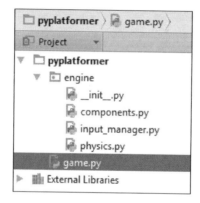

The pyplatformer/game.py script contains the game logic, and thanks to the micro-framework that we have developed, it will consist of a dozen short classes only.

Developing PyPlatformer

With this architectural background, we can start crafting the custom components of our platformer game. The Component API may look simple, but it allows us to implement the functionality in a succinct manner.

Creating the platforms

Each platform of our game is nothing but a cube with a static rigid body. However, since we will create several instances with these components, it is convenient to define a class to avoid repeating this kind of instantiation:

```
class Platform(GameObject):
    def __init__(self, x, y, width, height):
        super(Platform, self).__init__(x, y)
        color = (0.2, 1, 0.5, 1)
        self.add_components(Cube(color, size=(width, height, 2)),
                            BoxCollider(width, height))
```

Adding pickups

In platformer games, it is common that the player is able to collect some items that give valuable resources. In our game, when the character hits one of these pickups, its ammo is incremented by five units.

To decorate this type of game object, we will add a component that rotates the attached game object around its *y* axis:

```
class Rotating(Component):
    speed = 50
    def update(self, dt):
        ax, ay, az = self.gameobject.rotation
        ay = (ay + self.speed * dt) % 360
        self.gameobject.rotation = ax, ay, az
```

Finally, we can define a GameObject subclass that wraps the instantiation of these components:

```
class Pickup(GameObject):
    def __init__(self, x, y):
        super(Pickup, self).__init__(x, y)
        self.tag = 'pickup'
        color = (1, 1, 0.5, 1)
        self.add_components(Cube(color, size=(1, 1, 1)),
                            Rotating(), BoxCollider(1, 1))
```

We use the tag attribute as a way of identifying its type. Thus, if we need to check the game object's type, we don't need to rely on the isinstance function and the hierarchy model.

Shooting!

When the player collides with one of these pickups, it is destroyed and it is no longer displayed on the scene. With a physics engine, this also means removing the game object and disabling its rigid body. Remember that we defined the `GameObject.remove()` method for this purpose.

To simulate the gradual disappearance of the object, we will decrease its scale until it does not become visible, and then we will remove it:

```
class Disappear(Component):
    def update(self, dt):
        self.gameobject.velocity = 0, 0
        s1, s2, s3 = map(lambda s: s - dt*2,
                         self.gameobject.scale)
        self.gameobject.scale = s1, s2, s3
        if s1 <= 0: self.gameobject.remove()
```

This component is attached dynamically to the pickup and forces its removal. The ability to shoot and collect these items is defined in the `Shooter` component:

```
class Shoot(Component):
    def on_collide(self, other, contacts):
        self.gameobject.remove()


class Shooter(Component):
    __slots__ = ['ammo']

    def __init__(self):
        self.ammo = 0


    def update(self, dt):
        if Input.get_key_down(K_SPACE) and self.ammo > 0:
            self.ammo -= 1
            d = 1 if self.gameobject.velocity.x > 0 else -1
            pos = self.gameobject.position
            shoot = GameObject(pos[0] + 1.5 * d, pos[1])
            shoot.tag = 'shoot'
            color = (1, 1, 0, 1)
            shoot.add_components(Sphere(0.3, color), Shoot(),
                                 SphereCollider(0.3, mass=0.1,
                                                is_static=False))
            shoot.apply_force(20 * direction, 0)
```

```
def on_collide(self, other, contacts):
    if other.tag == 'pickup':
        self.ammo += 5
        other.add_component(Disappear())
```

Each time the player shoots, a game object is instantiated and moves towards the current game object's direction. It has an auxiliary `Shoot` component. This component removes the `shoot` instance when it collides with other rigid bodies.

To decide which entities are affected by a player's shooting, we add a component that checks the colliding entity's tag and disappears if it is a `shoot`:

```
class Shootable(Component):
    def on_collide(self, other, contacts):
        if other.tag == 'shoot':
            self.gameobject.add_component(Disappear())
```

Now each enemy has the following components:

```
class Enemy(GameObject):
    def __init__(self, x, y):
        super(Enemy, self).__init__(x, y)
        self.tag = 'enemy'
        color = (1, 0.2, 0.2, 1)
        self.add_components(Sphere(1, color), Shootable(),
                            SphereCollider(1, is_static=False))
```

The Player class and its components

Apart from the rigid body and the `Shooter`, our player character has two main components:

- **Respawn**: This spawns the player in its initial position if it falls into the void or collides with an enemy. The following is an example of the `Respawn` class:

```
class Respawn(Component):
    __slots__ = ['limit', 'spawn_position']

    def __init__(self, limit=-15):
        self.limit = limit
        self.spawn_position = None

    def start(self):
        self.spawn_position = self.gameobject.position
```

```
    def update(self, dt):
        if self.gameobject.position[1] < self.limit:
            self.respawn()

    def on_collide(self, other, contacts):
        if other.tag == 'enemy':
            self.respawn()

    def respawn(self):
        self.gameobject.velocity = 0, 0
        self.gameobject.position = self.spawn_position
```

- **PlayerMovement**: This queries the input state and checks what forces can be applied to the character's rigid body to move it horizontally or make it jump. Here is an example of the `PlayerMovement` class:

```
class PlayerMovement(Component):
    __slots__ = ['can_jump']

    def __init__(self):
        self.can_jump = False

    def update(self, dt):
        d = Input.get_key(K_RIGHT) - Input.get_key(K_LEFT)
        self.gameobject.move(d * 5 * dt, 0)
        if Input.get_key(K_UP) and self.can_jump:
            self.can_jump = False
            self.gameobject.move(0, 8)

    def on_collide(self, other, contacts):
        self.can_jump |= any(c.normal.y < 0 for c in contacts)
```

 Note how we use the list of contact points to check whether the player has touched the ground, and then enable the jump movement again.

The `Player` class combines all of these components into a single entity:

```
class Player(GameObject):
    def __init__(self, x, y):
        super(Player, self).__init__(x, y)
        self.add_components(Sphere(1, (1, 1, 1, 1)),
                            PlayerMovement(), Respawn(),
                            Shooter(), Camera(10, 20),
                            SphereCollider(1, is_static=False))
```

The PyPlatformer class

Finally, we define a `Game` subclass that instantiates all of our game objects and places them in the scene:

```
class PyPlatformer(Game):
    def __init__(self):
        super(PyPlatformer, self).__init__('PyPlatformer')
        self.player = Player(-2, 0)
        self.light = GameObject(0, 10, 0)
        self.light.add_component(Light(GL_LIGHT0))
        self.ground = [
            # Platform 1
            Platform(3, -2, 30, 1),
            Platform(-11, 3, 2, 9),
            Platform(8, 0, 2, 3),
            # Platform 2 & 3
            Platform(23, 0, 6, 1),
            Platform(40, 2, 24, 1),
            # Platform 4 & 5
            Platform(60, 3, 8, 1),
            Platform(84, 4, 26, 1)
        ]
        self.pickup = Pickup(60, 5)
        self.enemies = [Enemy(40, 4), Enemy(90, 6)]


if __name__ == '__main__':
    game = PyPlatformer()
    game.mainloop()
```

You can check out all the game objects and components in the `pyplatformer/game.py` script.

Summary

In this chapter, you learned about the benefits of a component-based design and how it allows you to build small pieces that can be added, removed, and combined with several game objects.

Note that the most important exercise of this chapter is not how to implement a platformer game, but how it is possible to set up a component-based framework and provide the basic building blocks of a game.

With these foundations, you can add some basic functionality, such as moving the enemies and the platforms, displaying more information about the ammo, or keeping track of a score based on the number of lives lost and enemies destroyed.

As usual, the final version of this chapter's game is nothing but the starting point of a more complex application!

In the next chapter, we will interact with a real-word checkers game via a webcam. This application will be developed with OpenCV, a cross-platform computer vision library.

7
Augmenting a Board Game
with Computer Vision

Computer vision is the science and engineering of smart camera systems (or more broadly, smart image systems, since images can come from another source besides a camera). Examples of subtopics in computer vision include face recognition, license plate recognition, image classification (as used in Google's **Search by image**), motion capture (as used in Xbox Kinect games), and 3D scanning.

Computer vision, like game development, has become more accessible in recent years and is now almost a ubiquitous topic. "How can we leverage people's interest in cameras?" or "How can we leverage all the cameras that are in our building, our city, or our country?" is as natural a question as "How can we leverage people's interest in games and simulations?" and the implications extend beyond entertainment.

Cameras are everywhere. Many of them are attached to powerful host computers and networks. We live, work, and play amidst an army of digital eyes, including webcams, camera phones, camera-controlled game consoles and smart TVs, security cameras, drones, and satellites. Images of you may be captured, processed, or transmitted many times daily.

The songwriter John Lennon asked us to "imagine all the people living for today" but, for a moment, let's imagine all pixels instead. A single image may contain millions of pixels, amounting to more bytes of data than Leo Tolstoy's *War and Peace* (an epic 1500-page novel about Russian society during the Napoleonic Wars). A single camera may capture a video stream containing thousands of these epic-sized images per minute. Billions of cameras are active in the world. Networks and disk drives are congested with the accumulation of image data, and once an image is online, copies of it may remain in circulation indefinitely. When we use software to acquire, edit, analyze, and review streams of images, we may notice that the computer's CPU usage soars while its battery power plummets.

As game developers, we know that a good game engine simplifies a lot of optimization problems, such as batching sprites or 3D models to send to the GPU for rendering. Good computer vision libraries (and more broadly, good numeric and scientific libraries) also simplify a lot of optimization problems and help us conserve CPU usage and battery life while processing video input (or other large streams of data) in real time. Since the 1990s, computer vision libraries, like game engines, have become more numerous, faster, easier to use, and often free. This chapter leverages the following libraries to capture, process, and display images:

- **NumPy**: This is a numeric library, which we previously used in *Chapter 4, Steering Behaviors*. Its documentation is at `http://docs.scipy.org/doc/`.

- **OpenCV**: This is a cross-platform library for computational photography, computer vision, and machine learning. OpenCV's Python version represents images as NumPy arrays. However, beneath the Python layer, OpenCV is implemented in C++ code with a wide range of hardware-specific optimizations. Thanks to these optimizations, OpenCV functions tend to run faster than their NumPy equivalents. The OpenCV documentation is at `http://docs.opencv.org/`.

- **scikit-learn**: This is a machine learning library. It processes NumPy arrays. For its documentation, refer to `http://scikit-learn.org/stable/documentation.html`.

- **WxPython**: This is a cross-platform GUI framework. On each platform, WxPython is certain to have a native look and feel because it uses native GUI widgets (in comparison, many cross-platform GUI frameworks, such as Tkinter, use their own non-native widgets with a configurable "skin" that may emulate a native look). WxPython is a wrapper around a C++ library called WxWidgets. For WxPython's documentation, refer to `http://wxpython.org/onlinedocs.php`.

 Later in this chapter, in the *Setting up OpenCV and other dependencies* section, we will discuss the version requirements and setup steps for each library.

Following the pattern of other chapters in this book, we will apply computer vision to a classic game: checkers, also known as draughts. This board game has many variants from all cultures and all periods of history in the past 5,000 years. It is the grandfather of all strategy games. Across most variants, the game has the following features:

- There are two players, who are sometimes called **light** and **dark**.

- There are two kinds of playing pieces, sometimes called **pawns** and **kings**. A pawn is a short, circular playing piece. A king is a tall, circular playing piece made by stacking two pawns.

- The board is a grid of alternating light and dark squares. Pieces may only occupy the dark squares. The size of the grid depends on the variant of the game.

- At the start of the game, each player has an army of pawns, occupying multiple adjacent rows on one side of the board. The two armies start on opposite sides of the board with two vacant rows between them.

- A piece may capture an opposing piece by jumping over it into an unoccupied square. A piece may make multiple jumps in one turn.

- On reaching the farthest row, a pawn is promoted to a king.

- The difference between a pawn and a king depends on the variant. In some variants, only a king can move back toward its starting side. Moreover, in some variants, a pawn can cross only one unoccupied square at a time while a king can cross multiple unoccupied squares. The latter are called **flying kings**.

For descriptions of many international variants of checkers, or draughts, refer to `https://en.wikipedia.org/wiki/Draughts`.

We will build an application that monitors a real-world game of checkers via a webcam. The application will detect a checkerboard and classify each square as an empty square, a light pawn, a light king, a dark pawn, or a dark king. Furthermore, the application will alter the webcam's images to create a bird's-eye view of the board, with labels to show the results of the classification. This is a simple case of **augmented reality**, meaning that the application applies special effects and annotations to a real-time view of a real-world object. We will call this application, quite simply, *Checkers*.

The completed project for this chapter can be downloaded from `http://nummist.com/opencv/4507_07.zip`, and any FAQ and errata can be found at `http://nummist.com/opencv`.

Planning the Checkers application

Let's give further thought to the real-world scene that our *Checkers* program will expect and the virtual scene it will create. Consider the following close-up photograph, showing part of an 8 x 8 checkerboard. From the top-left corner to right-hand side, we see a light king, a light pawn, a dark pawn, and a dark king.

This checkerboard is just a sheet of matte paper on which black and white squares are printed (the paper is glued to a foam board to make it rigid). The playing pieces happen to be poker chips—red chips for the dark side and gray chips for the light side. A stack of two poker chips is a pawn, while a stack of four is a king. As this example suggests, people may play checkers with homemade or improvised sets. There is no guarantee that two checkers sets will look alike, so we will try to avoid rigid assumptions about the color scheme. However, high contrast is generally helpful in computer vision, and this example is ideal because it uses four contrasting colors for dark squares, light squares, dark pieces, and light pieces.

We will assume that a light border surrounds the checkerboard (see the preceding image). This assumption makes it easier to detect the board's edge.

Look carefully at the white squares to the left of the kings. Since the kings are taller than the pawns, the kings cast longer shadows into adjacent light squares. We will rely on this observation to differentiate between pawns and kings. Importantly, in a bird's-eye view of the board, the heights of the playing pieces will not be visible but the shadows will be. We will assume that the shadows are approximately orthogonal (not diagonal), and are sufficiently long to reach an adjacent square.

To further simplify our computer vision work, we will require that the camera and checkerboard remain stationary relative to each other. The camera should have a view of the entire board plus a small margin. To achieve this, the webcam will need to be approximately 2 feet, or 0.6 meters, away from the board (however, the exact requirement will vary depending on the webcam's field of view and the board's size). As seen in the following photograph, a tripod is a good way to keep the webcam stationary in a high position from where it can view the whole board:

As the following screenshot shows, our *Checkers* application will display both the unmodified camera view (left) and an idealized bird's-eye view (right):

The bird's-eye view contains annotations, or in other words, text for showing the classification results. The annotation *1* means a dark pawn, *11* a dark king, *2* a light pawn, and *22* a light king. A lack of annotation means an empty square.

Note the GUI widgets at the bottom of the screenshot. These controls will enable the user to adjust certain parameters of our checkerboard detector and square classifier. Specifically, the following adjustments will be supported:

- **Rotate board CCW**: Click on this button to rotate the bird's-eye view 90 degrees counterclockwise (CCW)

- **Flip board X**: Click on this button to flip the bird's-eye view horizontally

- **Flip board Y**: Click on this button to flip the bird's-eye view vertically

- **Shadow direction**: Select one of the radio buttons—**up, left, down,** or **right**— to specify the direction of the kings' shadows in the bird's-eye view

- **Empty threshold**: Move this slider to the left to classify more squares as nonempty, or to the right to classify more squares as empty

- **Player threshold**: Move this slider to the left to classify more pieces as light, or to the right to classify more pieces as dark

- **Shadow threshold**: Move this slider to the left to classify more pieces as kings, or to the right to classify more pieces as pawns

We will divide our implementation of the `Checkers` application into six
Python modules:

- `Checkers.py`: This module implements the GUI using WxPython.
- `CheckersModel.py`: This module uses OpenCV, NumPy, and scikit-learn to capture, analyze, and augment images of a checkers game in real time.
- `WxUtils.py`: This module provides a utility function to convert images from OpenCV formats to a displayable WxPython format. The implementation includes a workaround for a WxPython bug that affects first-generation Raspberry Pi computers.
- `ResizeUtils.py`: Using OpenCV, this module provides a utility function to try to set a camera's resolution and return the actual resolution.
- `ColorUtils.py`: Using NumPy, this module provides utility functions to extract a color channel (such as the red component of an image) and quantify differences the between colors.
- `CVBackwardCompat.py`: This module provides aliases so that things in OpenCV 2.x appear to have the same names as their equivalents in OpenCV 3.x.

Before we write any of these modules, let's set up the dependencies.

Setting up OpenCV and other dependencies

This chapter's project will work with OpenCV 2.x or 3.x and Python 2.7 or 3.4. Note that OpenCV 2.x does not support Python 3.x. However, on most Linux systems, it is more convenient to install OpenCV 2.x (and use Python 2.7) because OpenCV 3.x does not have binary packages for most Linux systems yet.

The following subsections cover only the simplest ways to set up our dependencies on Windows, Mac, and several Linux distributions. Other approaches (and other Unix-like platforms) can also work. For example, advanced users may wish to configure and build OpenCV 3.0's source code on Linux systems that do not yet have prepackaged builds of OpenCV 3.x. For guidance on alternative setups, refer to one of Packt Publishing's dedicated books on OpenCV, such as *Learning OpenCV 3 Computer Vision with Python* by Joe Minichino and Joseph Howse.

Windows

Christoph Gohlke, from the University of California, Irvine, provides many reliable prebuilt versions of scientific Python libraries for Windows. Go to his download site at `http://www.lfd.uci.edu/~gohlke/pythonlibs/`. If you had not installed NumPy in *Chapter 4, Steering behaviors*, get the latest NumPy+MKL `whl` file from Gohlke's site (MKL is an Intel Math Kernel Library that provides optimizations). At the time of writing this book, it is one of the following:

- Python 2.7, 32-bit: `numpy-1.9.2+mkl-cp27-none-win32.whl`
- Python 2.7, 64-bit: `numpy-1.9.2+mkl-cp27-none-win_amd64.whl`
- Python 3.4, 32-bit: `numpy-1.9.2+mkl-cp34-none-win32.whl`
- Python 3.4, 64-bit: `numpy-1.9.2+mkl-cp34-none-win_amd64.whl`

Open Command Prompt and use `pip` to install NumPy from the wheel file. The relevant command will be something like this:

```
$ pip install numpy-1.9.2+mkl-cp27-none-win32.whl
```

The output from this command should include **Successfully installed numpy-1.9.2+mkl** or a similar line.

 If you run into problems later while importing modules from OpenCV or scikit-learn, try uninstalling any previous version of NumPy from *Chapter 4, Steering behaviors* and using the latest NumPy+MKL `whl` file from Gohlke's site.

Similarly, get Gohlke's latest `whl` file for scikit-learn and install it with `pip`. At the time of writing this book, it is one of the following:

- Python 2.7, 32-bit: `scikit_learn-0.16.1-cp27-none-win32.whl`
- Python 2.7, 64-bit: `scikit_learn-0.16.1-cp27-none-win_amd64.whl`
- Python 3.4, 32-bit: `scikit_learn-0.16.1-cp34-none-win32.whl`
- Python 3.4, 64-bit: `scikit_learn-0.16.1-cp34-none-win_amd64.whl`

Also, at the time of writing this book, Gohlke offers downloads of OpenCV 2.4 for Python 2.7 and OpenCV 3.0 for Python 3.4. The following are the latest versions:

- Python 2.7, 32-bit: `opencv_python-2.4.11-cp27-none-win32.whl`
- Python 2.7, 64-bit: `opencv_python-2.4.11-cp27-none-win_amd64.whl`
- Python 3.4, 32-bit: `opencv_python-3.0.0-cp34-none-win32.whl`
- Python 3.4, 64-bit: `opencv_python-3.0.0-cp34-none-win_amd64.whl`

If you are satisfied with using Gohlke's latest build of OpenCV, download the `whl` file and install it with `pip`.

Alternatively, to get OpenCV 3.x with Python 2.7 bindings, we can download an official build from the OpenCV site and perform some installation steps manually. The available downloads of OpenCV are listed at `http://opencv.org/downloads.html`. Get the latest version for Windows. At the time of writing this book, the latest file is called `opencv-3.0.0.exe`, and it includes prebuilt bindings for Python 2.7 but not 3.4. Run it, and when prompted, enter the folder into which you want to extract OpenCV. We will refer to this location as `<opencv_unzip_path>`. Among other things, the extracted subfolders contain the `pyd` and `dll` files, which are compiled library files that the Python interpreter can load at runtime. Next, we must ensure that Python can find these files.

Copy one of the following `pyd` files to the Python `site-packages` folder:

- Python 2.7, 32-bit: `<opencv_unzip_path>/opencv/build/python/x86/cv2.pyd`
- Python 2.7, 64-bit: `<opencv_unzip_path>/opencv/build/python/x64/cv2.pyd`

 Typically, the Python 2.7 `site-packages` folder would be located at `C:\Python27\Lib\site-packages`.

Now, edit the system's `Path` variable to include one of the following folders (which contain `dll` files of OpenCV and some of its dependencies):

- Python 2.7, 32-bit: `<opencv_unzip_path>/build/x86/vc12/bin`
- Python 2.7, 64-bit: `<opencv_unzip_path>/build/x64/vc12/bin`

 The `Path` variable can be edited by going to **Control Panel | System and Security | System | Advanced system settings | Environment Variables....** Edit the existing value of `Path` by appending something like; `<opencv_unzip_path>/build/x86/vc12/bin`. Note the use of the semicolon as a separator between paths.

Finally, we require wxPython. For Python 2.7, wxPython installers are available at `http://wxpython.org/download.php`. Download and run the latest installer. At the time of writing, it is one of the following `exe` files:

- Python 2.7, 32-bit: `wxPython3.0-win32-3.0.2.0-py27.exe`
- Python 2.7, 64-bit: `wxPython3.0-win64-3.0.2.0-py27.exe`

For Python 3.4, we must use wxPython Phoenix, which is a more actively developed fork of wxPython. Snapshot builds of wxPython Phoenix are listed at `http://wxpython.org/Phoenix/snapshot-builds/`. Download the latest `whl` file for Python 3.4 on Windows, and install it with pip. At the time of writing this book, it is one of the following:

- Python 3.4, 32-bit: `wxPython_Phoenix-3.0.3.dev1764+9289a7c-cp34-none-win32.whl`

- Python 3.4, 64-bit: `wxPython_Phoenix-3.0.3.dev1764+9289a7c-cp34-none-win_amd64.whl`

Now, we have all the necessary dependencies for developing our project on Windows.

Mac

The MacPorts package manager provides an easy command-line tool to configure, build, and install open source software, such as OpenCV. MacPorts itself is an open source community project, but it depends on Apple's Xcode development environment, including the **Xcode Command Line Tools**. To set up Xcode, the Xcode Command Line Tools, and then MacPorts, follow the instructions given at `https://www.macports.org/install.php`.

Once MacPorts is set up, we can open the terminal and start installing packages, also known as **ports**. A typical installation command has the following format:

```
$ sudo port install <package> +<variant_0> +<variant_1> ...
```

The variants are alternative configurations of the port. For example, OpenCV can be configured to build its Python bindings and to use optimizations for certain pieces of hardware. These optimizations add more dependencies to OpenCV but may make its functions run faster. We will tell OpenCV to optimize itself via three frameworks: Eigen (for CPU vector processing), Intel **Thread Building Blocks** (TBB, for CPU multiprocessing), and OpenCL (for GPU multiprocessing). The OpenCL optimizations are not used by the Python interface, but it is good to have them just in case you work in future with OpenCV in other languages.

To search for ports by name, run a command such as the following:

```
$ port list *cv*
```

The preceding command will list all ports whose names contain cv, notably the opencv port. To list the variants of a port, run a command such as this:

```
$ port variants opencv
```

To install OpenCV for Python 2.7, run the following command in the terminal:

```
$ sudo port install opencv +python27 +eigen +tbb +opencl
```

Alternatively, to install it for Python 3.4, run this command:

```
$ sudo port install opencv +python34 +eigen +tbb +opencl
```

Note that opencv +python27 depends on python27 and py27-numpy, while opencv +python34 depends on python34 and py34-numpy. Thus, the relevant Python version and NumPy version are also installed. All MacPorts Python installations are separate from Mac's built-in Python installation (sometimes called **Apple Python**). To use the MacPorts Python 2.7 installation as your default Python interpreter, run the following command:

```
$ sudo port select python python27
```

Alternatively, to make the MacPorts Python 3.4 installation your default Python interpreter, run this command:

```
$ sudo port select python python34
```

If it ever becomes necessary to make Apple Python the default again, run a command such as the following:

```
$ port select python python27-apple
```

For Python 2.7, here is a command that serves to install scikit-learn:

```
$ sudo port install py27-scikit-learn
```

Similarly, for Python 3.4, the following command installs scikit-learn:

```
$ sudo port install py34-scikit-learn
```

To install wxPython for Python 2.7, run this command:

```
$ sudo port install py27-wxpython-3.0
```

For Python 3.x, we need to use wxPython Phoenix, which is a more actively developed fork of wxPython. At the time of writing this book, MacPorts does not contain any wxPython Phoenix packages, so we will first set up `pip` and then use it to install the latest snapshot build of wxPython Phoenix. To install `pip` for Python 3.4, run the following command:

```
$ sudo port install py34-pip
```

We can make the newly installed `pip` the default `pip` executable:

```
$ sudo port select pip pip34
```

Snapshot builds of wxPython Phoenix are listed at `http://wxpython.org/Phoenix/snapshot-builds/`. Download the latest `whl` file for Python 3.4 on Mac. At the time of writing this book, it is `wxPython_Phoenix-3.0.3.dev1764+9289a7c-cp34-cp34m-macosx_10_6_intel.whl`. To install this package, run a command such as the following:

```
$ sudo pip install wxPython_Phoenix-3.0.3.dev1764+9289a7c-cp34-cp34m-macosx_10_6_intel.whl
```

The output from this command should include **Successfully installed wxPython-Phoenix-3.0.3.dev1764+9289a7c** or a similar line.

Now, we have all the necessary dependencies for developing our project on Mac.

Debian and its derivatives, including Raspbian, Ubuntu, and Linux Mint

For Python 2.7, the required libraries are in the standard repository. To install them, open the terminal and run the following command:

```
$ sudo apt-get install python-opencv python-scikits-learn python-wxgtk2.8
```

Note that the `python-opencv` package depends on the `python-numpy` package, so `python-numpy` will also be installed.

As an alternative, you can install wxPython Phoenix instead of the `python-wxgtk2.8` package. To set up wxPython Phoenix and its dependencies, try the following commands:

```
$ sudo apt-get install libwxbase3.0-dev libwxgtk3.0-dev wx-common
libwebkit-dev libwxgtk-webview3.0-dev wx3.0-examples wx3.0-headers wx3.0-
i18n libwxgtk-media3.0-dev
$ pip install --upgrade --pre -f http://wxpython.org/Phoenix/snapshot-
builds/ --trusted-host wxpython.org wxPython_Phoenix
```

However, if in doubt, just use the `python-wxgtk2.8` package.

Fedora and its derivatives, including RHEL and CentOS

For Python 2.7, the required libraries are in the standard repository. To install them, open the terminal and run the following command:

```
$ sudo yum install opencv-python python-scikit-learn wxPython
```

Note that the `opencv-python` package depends on the `numpy` package, so `numpy` will also be installed.

OpenSUSE and its derivatives

Again, for Python 2.7, the required libraries are in the standard repository. To install them, open the terminal and run the following command:

```
$ sudo yum install python-opencv python-scikit-learn python-wxWidgets
```

Note that the `python-opencv` package depends on the `python-numpy` package, so `python-numpy` will also be installed.

Supporting multiple versions of OpenCV

OpenCV 2.x and OpenCV 3.x both use the name `cv2` for their top-level Python module. However, inside this module, some classes, functions, and constants have been renamed in OpenCV 3.x. Moreover, some functionality is entirely new in OpenCV 3.x, but our project relies only on functionality that is present in both major versions.

To bridge a few of the naming differences between versions 2.x and 3.x, we create a module, `CVBackwardCompat`. It begins by importing `cv2`:

```
import cv2
```

OpenCV's version string is stored in `cv2.__version__`. For example, its value may be `2.4.11` or `3.0.0`. We can use the following line of code to get the major version number as an integer, such as `2` or `3`:

```
CV_MAJOR_VERSION = int(cv2.__version__.split('.')[0])
```

For OpenCV 2.x (or earlier), we will inject new names into the imported `cv2` module so that all the necessary OpenCV 3.x names will be present. Specifically, we need to create aliases for several constants that have new names in OpenCV 3.x, as seen in the following code:

```
if CV_MAJOR_VERSION < 3:
    # Create aliases to make parts of the OpenCV 2.x library
    # forward-compatible.
    cv2.LINE_AA = cv2.CV_AA
    cv2.CAP_PROP_FRAME_WIDTH = cv2.cv.CV_CAP_PROP_FRAME_WIDTH
    cv2.CAP_PROP_FRAME_HEIGHT = cv2.cv.CV_CAP_PROP_FRAME_HEIGHT
    cv2.FILLED = cv2.cv.CV_FILLED
```

This is the entire implementation of `CVBackwardCompat`. Our other modules will be able to import the `CVBackwardCompat` instance of `cv2` and use any of the aliases that we may have injected. We will see an example in the next module—`ResizeUtils`.

Configuring cameras

OpenCV provides a class, called `cv2.VideoCapture`, that represents a stream of images from either a video file or a camera. This class has methods such as `read(image)` for exposing the stream's next image as a NumPy array. It also has the `get(propId)` and `set(propId, value)` methods for accessing properties such as the width and height (in pixels), color format, and frame rate. The valid properties and values may depend on the system's video codecs or camera drivers.

Across cameras, the default property values may differ dramatically. For example, one camera might default to an image size of 640 x 480, while another may default to 1920 x 1080. For greater predictability, we should try to set crucial parameters rather than rely on the defaults. Let's create a module called `ResizeUtils` containing a utility function to configure the image size.

The `ResizeUtils` module begins by importing the `CVBackwardCompat` instance of `cv2`, which may contain aliases (depending on the OpenCV version). Here is the import statement:

```
from CVBackwardCompat import cv2
```

The property IDs for width and height are stored in constants called cv2.CAP_PROP_ FRAME_WIDTH and cv2.CAP_PROP_FRAME_HEIGHT, respectively (referring to the previous section, note that the constants' original names in OpenCV 2.x were cv2. cv.CV_CAP_PROP_FRAME_WIDTH and cv2.cv.CV_CAP_PROP_FRAME_HEIGHT, but we created aliases to match the OpenCV 3.x names). Note the use of these constants in the following implementation of the utility function:

```
def cvResizeCapture(capture, preferredSize):
    # Try to set the requested dimensions.
    w, h = preferredSize
    successW = capture.set(cv2.CAP_PROP_FRAME_WIDTH, w)
    successH = capture.set(cv2.CAP_PROP_FRAME_HEIGHT, h)
    if successW and successH:
        # The requested dimensions were successfully set.
        # Return the requested dimensions.
        return preferredSize
    # The requested dimensions might not have been set.
    # Return the actual dimensions.
    w = capture.get(cv2.CAP_PROP_FRAME_WIDTH)
    h = capture.get(cv2.CAP_PROP_FRAME_HEIGHT)
    return (w, h)
```

As arguments, the function takes a cv2.VideoCapture object called capture and a two-dimensional tuple called preferredSize. We try to configure capture to use the preferred width and height in preferredSize. The preferred dimensions may or may not be supported, so as with the feedback, we return a tuple of the actual width and height.

The ResizeUtils module will be useful for our CheckersModel module, as CheckersModel is responsible for instantiating and reading from cv2.VideoCapture.

Working with colors

Normally, when OpenCV obtains an image from a file or camera, it puts the image in the blue-green-red (BGR) color format. More specifically, the image is a 3D NumPy array in which image[y][x][0] is a pixel's blue value (in the range of 0 to 255), image[y][x][1] is its green value, and image[y][x][2] is its red value. The y and x indices start from the top-left corner of the image. If we convert an image into grayscale, it becomes a 2D NumPy array, in which image[y][x] is a pixel's grayscale value.

Let's write some utility functions in the `ColorUtils` module to work with color data. Our functions will use Python's standard `math` module and NumPy, as seen in the following `import` statements:

```
import math
import numpy
```

Let's write a function that allows us to copy a single color channel from a source image (which is in BGR format) to a destination image (which is in grayscale format). If the specified destination image is `None` or its format is wrong, our function will create it. To copy the channel, we just take a flat view of the source image, slice it with a stride of 3, and assign the result to a full slice of the destination image, as seen in the following implementation:

```
def extractChannel(src, channel, dst):
    dstShape = src.shape[:2]
    if dst is None or dst.shape != dstShape or \
            dst.dtype != numpy.uint8:
        dst = numpy.empty(dstShape, numpy.uint8)
    dst[:] = src.flatten()[channel::3].reshape(dstShape)
    return dst
```

For typical checkerboards under typical lighting conditions, the red channel shows a high contrast between dark and light squares. Later, we will use this observation to our advantage.

On the other hand, parts of our analysis will rely on full colors instead of only one channel. We will need to quantify the contrast or **distance** between two BGR colors in order to decide whether a square contains a light piece, a dark piece, a shadow, or nothing. A naïve approach is to use the Euclidean distance, which would be implemented like this:

```
def colorDist(color0, color1):
    return math.sqrt(
        (color0[0] - color1[0]) ** 2 +
        (color0[1] - color1[1]) ** 2 +
        (color0[2] - color1[2]) ** 2)
```

However, this approach assumes that all color channels have the same scale and the scale is linear. This assumption defies common sense. For example, most people would agree that the color amber (*b=0, g=191, r=255*) is not a shade of red (*b=0, g=0, r=255*) but that the color emerald (*b=191, g=255, r=0*) *is* a shade of green (*b=0, g=255, r=0*), even though these two pairings represent the same Euclidean distance (*191*). Many alternative formulations assume that the channels are still linear but have different scales—typically, they assume that green has the biggest unit, followed by red, and then blue. These formulations yield high contrast between yellow and blue (for example, between sunlight and shade), and yet yield low contrast between shades of blue. This is still rather unsatisfactory because most people are good at distinguishing shades of blue. Thiadmer Riemersma compares several distance formulations at http://www.compuphase.com/cmetric.htm, and proposes an alternative in which the green scale is linear while the red and blue scales are nonlinear, with red differences having more weight in comparisons of reddish colors and blue differences having more weight in comparisons of non-reddish colors. Let's replace our previous colorDist function with the following implementation of Riemersma's method:

```
def colorDist(color0, color1):
    # Calculate a red-weighted color distance, as described
    # here: http://www.compuphase.com/cmetric.htm
    rMean = int((color0[2] + color1[2]) / 2)
    rDiff = int(color0[2] - color1[2])
    gDiff = int(color0[1] - color1[1])
    bDiff = int(color0[0] - color1[0])
    return math.sqrt(
        (((512 + rMean) * rDiff * rDiff) >> 8) +
        4 * gDiff * gDiff +
        (((767 - rMean) * bDiff * bDiff) >> 8))
```

Based on the preceding formula, the distance between black and white is approximately 764.8. The scale of this distance is not intuitive. We might prefer to work with normalized values, whereby the normalized distance between black and white is defined as 1.0. The following function returns a normalized color distance:

```
def normColorDist(color0, color1):
    # Normalize based on the distance between (0, 0, 0) and
    # (255, 255, 255).
    return colorDist(color0, color1) / 764.8333151739665
```

Now we have sufficient utility functions to support our upcoming implementation of the CheckersModel module, which will capture and analyze images.

Building the analyzer

The `CheckersModel` module is the eyes and the brain of our project. It brings together everything except the GUI. Specifically, it depends on NumPy, OpenCV, scikit-learn, and our `ColorUtils` and `ResizeUtils` modules, as reflected in the following `import` statements:

```
import numpy
import sklearn.cluster
from CVBackwardCompat import cv2

import ColorUtils
import ResizeUtils
```

> Although we are combining image capturing and analysis into one module, they are arguably distinct responsibilities. For this project, they share a dependency on OpenCV. However, in a future project, you might capture images from a camera that requires another library, or from an entirely different type of source, such as a network. You might even support a wide variety of capturing techniques in one project. Whenever you feel that image capture is a complex problem in its own right, consider dedicating at least one separate module to it.

To make our code more readable, we will define several constants in this module. These constants represent the possible states of the board's rotation, the shadows' direction, and each square's classification. Here are their definitions:

```
ROTATION_0 = 0
ROTATION_CCW_90 = 1
ROTATION_180 = 2
ROTATION_CCW_270 = 3

DIRECTION_UP = 0
DIRECTION_LEFT = 1
DIRECTION_DOWN = 2
DIRECTION_RIGHT = 3

SQUARE_STATUS_UNKNOWN = -1
SQUARE_STATUS_EMPTY = 0
SQUARE_STATUS_PAWN_PLAYER_1 = 1
SQUARE_STATUS_KING_PLAYER_1 = 11
SQUARE_STATUS_PAWN_PLAYER_2 = 2
SQUARE_STATUS_KING_PLAYER_2 = 22
```

This module will also contain the CheckersModel class, declared like this:

```
class CheckersModel(object):
```

Note that we have made CheckersModel a subclass of object. This is important for Python 2.x compatibility because we are going to use property getter and setter methods, as discussed in the next subsection. Unlike Python 3.x, Python 2.x does not support accessor methods in all classes, but rather only in subclasses of object.

Providing access to the images and classification results

The member variables of the CheckersModel class will include current images of the scene (that is, everything that the webcam can see) in BGR and grayscale, as well as a current image of the board in BGR. Unlike the scene, the board will be a bird's-eye view and may contain text in order to show the classification results. We will provide property getters so that other modules may read the images and their sizes, as seen in the following code:

```
@property
def sceneSize(self):
    return self._sceneSize
@property
def scene(self):
    return self._scene
@property
def sceneGray(self):
    return self._sceneGray
@property
def boardSize(self):
    return self._boardSize
@property
def board(self):
    return self._board
```

Property getters and setters simply provide a shorthand notation so that a method looks like a non-callable variable. Here is an example that demonstrates how to use a property getter:

```
bm = BoardModel()

scene = bm.scene  # Calls getter, bm.scene()
```

Here, we have implemented only a getter and not a setter because other modules should not set the images. Thus, a piece of code such as the following will produce an error:

```
bm.scene = None  # Calls setter, bm.scene(None)

# Error! There is no such setter.
```

The next subsection, *Providing access to parameters for the user to configure*, will give examples on how to implement setter methods.

We also provide a getter for the classification results as a 2D NumPy array:

```
@property
def squareStatuses(self):
    return self._squareStatuses
```

For example, if Player 1 has a king in the top-left corner of the board, boardModel. squareStatuses[0, 0] will be 11 (the value of the SQUARE_STATUS_KING_ PLAYER_1 constant, which we defined earlier).

All the aforementioned properties represent the results of the CheckersModel module's work, so other modules should treat them as read-only (and thus they have only getters, not setters). Next, let's consider other properties that represent the parameters of the CheckersModel module's work, and have both getters and setters so that other modules may reconfigure them.

Providing access to parameters for the user to configure

To understand *why* CheckersModel offers parameters that are reconfigurable at runtime, let's look at a preview of the things that we will *not* automate in this project:

- The bird's-eye view of the checkerboard may be rotated and flipped in a way different from what the user expects. This problem is discussed in the *Creating and analyzing the bird's-eye view of the board* subsection. We allow the user to specify a different rotation (0, 90, 180, or 270 degrees) and flip (X, Y, neither, or both).

- The shadows' direction is not detected automatically. By default, we assume that the shadows' direction is up (negative *y*). We allow the user to specify a direction (up, right, down, or left).
- To classify the contents of the squares, we compare the two dominant colors in the square, and this comparison relies on certain threshold values. For some lighting conditions and some colors of checkers sets, the default thresholds might not be appropriate. We allow the user to specify different thresholds. The precise meaning of each threshold is discussed in the *Analyzing the dominant colors in a square* subsection.

The board's rotation is expressed as an integer, corresponding to one of the constants that we declared at the start of this module. The following code implements the getters and setters for the rotation, and the setter uses the modulus operator to ensure that the rotations wrap around:

```
@property
def boardRotation(self):
    return self._boardRotation
@boardRotation.setter
def boardRotation(self, value):
    self._boardRotation = value % 4
```

The direction of the shadows is a similar property:

```
@property
def shadowDirection(self):
    return self._shadowDirection
@shadowDirection.setter
def shadowDirection(self, value):
    self._shadowDirection = value % 4
```

The thresholds and flip directions do not require any special logic in a getter or setter, so we will simply implement them as plain old member variables. We can see their declarations in the following code, which is the start of the class's initializer:

```
def __init__(self, patternSize=(7, 7), cameraDeviceID=0,
             sceneSize=(800, 600)):

    self.emptyFreqThreshold = 0.3
    self.playerDistThreshold = 0.4
    self.shadowDistThreshold = 0.45

    self._boardRotation = ROTATION_0
    self.flipBoardX = False
    self.flipBoardY = False
    self._shadowDirection = DIRECTION_UP
```

Let's proceed to look at the rest of the member variables and initialization code.

Initializing the entire model of the game

As we have previously discussed, the role of the `CheckersModel` class is to produce images of the scene and board and classify the contents of each square. The remainder of the `__init__` method declares variables that pertain to imaging and classification.

The images of the scene and board will initially be None, as seen here:

```
self._scene = None
self._sceneGray = None
self._board = None
```

Looking back at the previous subsection, note that `patternSize` is one of the initializer's arguments. This variable refers to the number of internal corners in the board, such as (7, 7) in a standard American checkerboard with eight rows and eight columns. Later, we will see that the number of internal corners is important for certain OpenCV functions. Let's put the corner dimensions and count into the member variables, like this:

```
self._patternSize = patternSize
self._numCorners = patternSize[0] * patternSize[1]
```

Later, as the steps toward classification, we will measure the frequency and distance of the two dominant colors in each square. This task is discussed in the *Analyzing the dominant colors in a square* subsection. For now, we will only create empty NumPy arrays for this data:

```
self._squareFreqs = numpy.empty(
        (patternSize[1] + 1, patternSize[0] + 1),
        numpy.float32)
self._squareDists = numpy.empty(
        (patternSize[1] + 1, patternSize[0] + 1),
        numpy.float32)
```

Similarly, we will create a NumPy array for the results of classification, and we will fill in this array with the SQUARE_STATUS_UNKNOWN value (which we previously defined as -1):

```
self._squareStatuses = numpy.empty(
        (patternSize[1] + 1, patternSize[0] + 1),
        numpy.int8)
self._squareStatuses.fill(SQUARE_STATUS_UNKNOWN)
```

To find each square's dominant colors, we will rely on a class in scikit-learn called `sklearn.cluster.MiniBatchKMeans`. This class represents a statistical process called **k-means clustering**, which separates data into a given number of groups and finds the centroid of each group. For now, we only need to construct an instance of the class with a single argument, `n_clusters`, which indicates the number of groups that the clusterer will distinguish (2 in this case, because we want to know the two dominant colors):

```
self._clusterer = sklearn.cluster.MiniBatchKMeans(2)
```

To support webcam input, we will create a `VideoCapture` object and set its capture dimensions using our utility function from the `ResizeUtils` module:

```
self._capture = cv2.VideoCapture(cameraDeviceID)
self._sceneSize = ResizeUtils.cvResizeCapture(
        self._capture, sceneSize)
w, h = self._sceneSize
```

Later, as we capture images, we will try to find the internal corners of the checkerboard, and we will store the successfully detected corners so that we do not have to perform this search from scratch for every frame. The following two member variables will hold the previously detected corners (initially `None`) and a grayscale image of the scene at the time of the previous detection (initially an empty image):

```
self._lastCorners = None
self._lastCornersSceneGray = numpy.empty(
        (h, w), numpy.uint8)
```

The scene's detected corner coordinates will imply a **homography** (a matrix that describes a difference in perspective) when we compare them with the known corner coordinates in a bird's-eye view of the board. Like the corners, the homography does not need to be recomputed for every frame, so we will store it in the following member variable (initially `None`):

```
self._boardHomography = None
```

We will arbitrarily stipulate that the bird's-eye view of the board will be no larger than the captured image of the scene. Starting from this constraint, we will calculate the size of a square and the board:

```
self._squareWidth = min(w, h) // (max(patternSize) + 1)
self._squareArea = self._squareWidth ** 2

self._boardSize = (
    (patternSize[0] + 1) * self._squareWidth,
    (patternSize[1] + 1) * self._squareWidth
)
```

Having determined the size of a square, we will calculate a set of corner coordinates for the bird's-eye view. We need the coordinates of only those internal corners where four squares meet. Later, in the *Detecting the board's corners and tracking their motion* subsection, we will compare these ideal coordinates to the internal corners of the checkerboard that are detected in the scene in order to find the homography. Here is our code for creating a list and then a NumPy array of evenly spaced corners:

```
self._referenceCorners = []
for x in range(patternSize[0]):
    for y in range(patternSize[1]):
        self._referenceCorners += [[x, y]]
self._referenceCorners = numpy.array(
        self._referenceCorners, numpy.float32)
self._referenceCorners *= self._squareWidth
self._referenceCorners += self._squareWidth
```

This concludes the initialization of the `CheckersModel` class. Next, let's consider how the images of the scene and board will change, along with the results of classification.

Updating the entire model of the game

Our `CheckersModel` class will provide the following `update` method, which other modules may call:

```
def update(self, drawCorners=False,
        drawSquareStatuses=True):
```

Specifically, the GUI application (in the `Checkers` module) will call this `update` method. Logically, the application is responsible for managing resources and ensuring that everything remains responsive, so it is in a better position to decide when an update should occur. The `update` method's `drawCorners` argument specifies whether the results of corner detection should be displayed in the scene. The `drawSquareStatuses` argument specifies whether the results of classification should be displayed in the bird's-eye view of the board.

The `update` method relies on several helper methods. First, we will call a helper that tries to capture a new image of the scene. If this fails, we return `False` to inform the caller that no update has occurred:

```
if not self._updateScene():
    return False  # Failure
```

We will proceed to search for the checkerboard in the scene. A successful search will produce a set of corner coordinates for the board's squares. Moreover, these coordinates will imply a homography. The following line of code calls a helper method that is responsible for finding the corners and a homography:

```
self._updateBoardHomography()
```

Next, we will call a helper method that is responsible for creating the bird's-eye view of the board as well as analyzing and classifying each square:

```
self._updateBoard()
```

At this point, the board detection and square classification are complete, but we may still need to display results depending on the drawCorners and drawSquareStatuses arguments. Conveniently, OpenCV provides a function, cv2.drawChessboardCorners(image, patternSize, corners, patternWasFound), to display a set of detected corners in a scene containing a chessboard or checkerboard. Here is the way we use it:

```
if drawCorners and self._lastCorners is not None:
    # Draw the board's grid.
    cv2.drawChessboardCorners(
            self._scene, self._patternSize,
            self._lastCorners, True)
```

We have another helper method for displaying the classification result in a given square. The following code shows how we iterate over squares and call the helper:

```
if drawSquareStatuses:
    for i in range(self._patternSize[0] + 1):
        for j in range(self._patternSize[1] + 1):
            self._drawSquareStatus(i, j)
```

At this point, the update has succeeded, and we return True to let the caller know that there are new results:

```
return True  # Success
```

Let's delve deeper into the helper methods' roles, starting with image capture.

Capturing and converting an image

OpenCV's VideoCapture class has a read(image) method. This method captures an image and writes it to the given destination array (if image is None or its format is wrong, a new array is created). The method returns a tuple, (retval, image), containing a boolean (True if the capture has succeeded) and then the image (either the old array or a newly created array). We use this method to try to capture a new scene from the camera. If this succeeds, we use our extractChannel utility function to get the red channel as a grayscale version of the scene. The following method performs these steps and returns a boolean to indicate success or failure:

```
def _updateScene(self):
    success, self._scene = self._capture.read(self._scene)
    if not success:
        return False  # Failure
    # Use the red channel as grayscale.
    self._sceneGray = ColorUtils.extractChannel(
            self._scene, 2, self._sceneGray)
    return True  # Success
```

Consider the following strip of images. The leftmost image represents the original scene in BGR color (though it will appear as grayscale in this book's print edition). This board's colors are burnt amber for the dark squares, ochre for the light squares, and burnt sienna for the border (this color scheme is quite common in checkerboards). The second, third, and fourth images (from left to right) represent the scene's blue, green, and red channels, respectively:

Note that the red channel captures the checkerboard brightly and with good contrast between lighter and darker squares. Moreover, the board's border appears quite light. This is good because we are soon going to use a detector that is optimized for a black-and-white board with a white border.

Detecting the board's corners and tracking their motion

We do not want to update the board's corners and homography in every frame, but only in frames where the board or camera has moved. This rule reduces the computational burden in most frames and allows us to keep a good detection result from a previous frame so that we do not require an unobstructed view of the board in every frame. Particularly, we can be relatively sure of getting good detection results when the board is empty, and we would want to keep these results for later frames in which the board is cluttered with pieces or with the players' moving hands.

Before finding new corners and the homography, let's look at tracking motion. Suppose we have detected a set of corners in a previous frame. Rather than searching the entire image for new corners, we can try to find the same corners at or near their previous locations. This idea—mapping frame-to-frame motion of individual points in an image—is called **optical flow**. OpenCV provides implementations of several optical flow techniques. We will use a technique called **pyramidal Lukas-Kanade**, which is implemented in the cv2.calcOpticalFlowPyrLK(prevImg, nextImg, prevPts) function. This function returns a tuple, (nextPts, status, error). Each of the tuple's elements is an array. The nextPts contains the points' estimated new coordinates. The status contains codes for indicating whether each estimate is valid (1, meaning the point was tracked) or invalid (0, meaning it was lost). Finally, error contains a measurement of dissimilarity between the pixels in the old and new neighborhoods for each point. A high average error across all points implies that everything looks different and, most likely, that the board or camera has moved. We apply this reasoning in the following code, which is the beginning of the _updateBoardHomography method:

```python
def _updateBoardHomography(self):

    if self._lastCorners is not None:
        corners, status, error = cv2.calcOpticalFlowPyrLK(
                self._lastCornersSceneGray,
                self._sceneGray, self._lastCorners, None)
        # Status is 1 if tracked, 0 if not tracked.
        numCornersTracked = sum(status)
        # If not tracked, error is invalid so set it to 0.
        error[:] = error * status
        meanError = (sum(error) / numCornersTracked)[0]
        if meanError < 4.0:
            # The board's old corners and homography are
            # still good enough.
            return
```

The threshold, `meanError < 4.0`, has been chosen experimentally. If you see that the estimate of the board's corners changes even when the board is still, try raising the threshold. Conversely, if you find that the estimate of the board's corners remains unchanged even when the board is moved, you may need to lower the threshold.

If we have not yet returned, it means that either there are no previously found corners, or the previously found corners are no longer valid (probably because the board or the camera has moved). Either way, we must search for new corners. OpenCV provides many general-purpose functions for finding any kind of corner, but conveniently, it also provides a specialized function for finding the corners of squares in a chessboard or a checkerboard. This function, `cv2.findChessboardCorners(image, patternSize)`, can find a board of any specified dimensions, even a non-square board. The `patternSize` argument specifies the number of internal corners, such as `(7, 7)` for a standard American checkerboard with eight rows and eight columns. This function returns a tuple, `(retval, corners)`, where `retval` is a Boolean (which is `True` if all the corners were found) and `corners` is a list of corner coordinates. It expects a checkerboard with pure black and pure white squares, but other color schemes may work depending on the strength of their contrast in the given grayscale image. Moreover, the function expects the board to have a light border, which makes it easier to find the corners of the outermost dark squares. The following code shows our usage of `findChessboardCorners`:

```
# Find the corners in the board's grid.
cornersWereFound, corners = cv2.findChessboardCorners(
        self._sceneGray, self._patternSize,
        flags=cv2.CALIB_CB_ADAPTIVE_THRESH)
```

Note that `findChessboardCorners` has an optional `flags` argument. We used a flag called `cv2.CALIB_CB_ADAPTIVE_THRESH`, which stands for **adaptive thresholding**. When this flag is set, the function attempts to compensate for the overall brightness of the image so that it does not necessarily require the squares to look really black or really white.

The small circles and lines shown in the following image are a visualization of the corners found using `findChessboardCorners`. They are drawn using the `drawChessboardCorners` function, which we covered in the previous subsection.

If the corners are found, we can convert their coordinates from a list to a
NumPy array. Then, we can compare the found coordinates with the reference
coordinates for a bird's-eye view (remember that we already initialized the
reference coordinates in the *Initializing the entire model of the game* subsection).
To compare the two sets of coordinates, we will use an OpenCV function called
cv2.findHomography(srcPoints, dstPoints, method). The optional method
argument represents a strategy to reject outliers (incongruous points that should not
be counted toward the result). The function returns a homography matrix, which
is a transformation that maps srcPoints to dstPoints with minimal error. The
following code demonstrates our use of findHomography:

```
if cornersWereFound:
    # Find the homography.
    corners = numpy.array(corners, numpy.float32)
    corners = corners.reshape(self._numCorners, 2)
    self._boardHomography, matches = cv2.findHomography(
            corners, self._referenceCorners, cv2.RANSAC)
    # Record the corners and their image.
    self._lastCorners = corners
    self._lastCornersSceneGray[:] = self._sceneGray
```

Note that we keep a copy of the grayscale image of the scene. The next time this method is called, we will compare the old and new grayscale scenes to track the corners' motion.

At this point, we may have found the board's homography, but we have not yet created an image to show the bird's-eye view. Let's tackle this task next.

Creating and analyzing the bird's-eye view of the board

If the board's corners and homography are found, we can transform the scene's perspective to produce a bird's-eye view of the board. The relevant function in OpenCV is `cv2.warpPerspective(src, M, dsize, dst)`, where M is the homography matrix and `dsize` is an arbitrary size for the output image. This function applies the homography matrix to change the perspective, and then it resizes and crops the result. Our `_updateBoard` method begins with the following code:

```
def _updateBoard(self):

    if self._boardHomography is not None:
        # Warp the board to obtain a bird's-eye view.
        self._board = cv2.warpPerspective(
            self._scene, self._boardHomography,
            self._boardSize, self._board)
```

The following pair of images shows the camera's view of the scene (left), and the resulting bird's-eye view of the board (right) after perspective transformation:

At this stage, the bird's-eye view might still need to be rotated and/or flipped to match the user's subjective perception of directions. The user is probably sitting on one side of the board and perceives this side as the "near" or "down" (positive y) side. The camera might be on the same side, any other side, or a diagonal! Moreover, depending on its drivers and configuration, the camera may even capture mirrored images. The findChessboardCorners function does not limit its search. As far as it is concerned, the scene *could* show an upside-down and mirrored chessboard, and this solution is as good as any other solution that puts a set of corners in the right places. We could inspect and edit the values in the _boardHomography matrix to enforce our own assumptions, but instead of this, we will let the user inspect the image and decide on any necessary changes.

Looking closely at the preceding pair of images, note that the board has a dark or blurry seam down the middle (it can fold here). The seam is approximately horizontal in the camera's view but vertical in the bird's-eye view. Moreover, the two views differ by a horizontal flip. A user might find these differences unintuitive.

OpenCV provides a function called cv2.flip(src, flipCode, dst) to flip an image in the manner specified by flipCode (-1 or less to flip both x and y coordinates, 0 to flip y coordinates, and 1 or greater to flip x coordinates). Another function, cv2.transpose(src, dst), serves to swap x and y coordinates with each other. A rotation of 90 or 270 degrees can be implemented as a combination of a transpose and a flip, while a rotation of 180 degrees can be implemented as a flip in both dimensions. Let's use these approaches in the following code to apply a specified flip and rotation:

```python
# Rotate and flip the board.
flipX = self.flipBoardX
flipY = self.flipBoardY
if self._boardRotation == ROTATION_CCW_90:
    cv2.transpose(self._board, self._board)
    flipX = not flipX
elif self._boardRotation == ROTATION_180:
    flipX = not flipX
    flipY = not flipY
elif self._boardRotation == ROTATION_CCW_270:
    cv2.transpose(self._board, self._board)
    flipY = not flipY
if flipX:
    if flipY:
        cv2.flip(self._board, -1, self._board)
    else:
        cv2.flip(self._board, 1, self._board)
elif flipY:
    cv2.flip(self._board, 0, self._board)
```

Later, we will ensure that user can set `boardRotation`, `flipBoardX`, and `flipBoardY` via the GUI. For example, the user can see the preceding pair of images and then make adjustments to produce the following pair of images instead:

Once the transformations are complete, we will iterate over all the squares and call a helper method to generate data about each square's color:

```
for i in range(self._patternSize[0] + 1):
    for j in range(self._patternSize[1] + 1):
        self._updateSquareData(i, j)
```

Then, we will iterate over all the squares again and call a helper method to update the classification of each square:

```
for i in range(self._patternSize[0] + 1):
    for j in range(self._patternSize[1] + 1):
        self._updateSquareStatus(i, j)
```

Note that a square's classification may rely on data about a neighboring square (since we may search for a shadow to distinguish a king from a pawn). This is why we analyze the colors of all the squares in one step and classify the squares in another step. Let's consider the analysis of colors now.

Analyzing the dominant colors in a square

Our _updateSquareData method takes a square's indices as arguments, and it begins by calculating the square's top-left and bottom-right pixel coordinates in the _board image, as seen in the following code:

```
def _updateSquareData(self, i, j):

    x0 = i * self._squareWidth
    x1 = x0 + self._squareWidth
    y0 = j * self._squareWidth
    y1 = y0 + self._squareWidth
```

Remember that we have a member variable called _clusterer. It is an instance of the sklearn.cluster.MiniBatchKMeans class. This class has a method, called fit(X), that classifies the data in X and stores the results in the member variables of MiniBatchKMeans. X must be a 2D NumPy array, so we must reshape the square's image data. For example, if a square has 75 x 75 pixels with three color channels, we will pass a view of the square as an array of shape (75*75, 3), not (75, 75, 3). The following code shows how we slice and reshape the square and pass it to the fit method:

```
# Find the two dominant colors in the square.
self._clusterer.fit(
        self._board[y0:y1, x0:x1].reshape(
                self._squareArea, 3))
```

The results of the color clustering are stored in _clusterer.centers and _clusterer.labels, which are NumPy arrays. The shape of centers is (2, 3), and it represents the two dominant BGR colors in the square. Meanwhile, labels is a one-dimensional array whose length is equal to the number of pixels in the square. Each value in labels is 0 if the pixel is clustered with the first dominant color, or 1 if the pixel is clustered with the second dominant color. Thus, the mean of labels represents the second color's frequency (the proportion of pixels that are clustered with this color). The following code shows how we can find the frequency of the less dominant color, as well as the normalized distance between the two dominant colors, based on the formula in our ColorUtils module:

```
# Find the proportion of the square's area that is
# occupied by the less dominant color.
freq = numpy.mean(self._clusterer.labels_)
if freq > 0.5:
    freq = 1.0 - freq

# Find the distance between the dominant colors.
```

```
dist = ColorUtils.normColorDist(
        self._clusterer.cluster_centers_[0],
        self._clusterer.cluster_centers_[1])

self._squareFreqs[j, i] = freq
self._squareDists[j, i] = dist
```

The frequency and distance enable us to talk about the square's colors at a much higher level of abstraction than raw channel values. For example, we may observe, "This square contains a big object that contrasts strongly with the background," (high frequency and high distance) without needing to search for any specific square color or playing piece color. Next, we will use such observations to classify the contents of a square.

Classifying the contents of a square

Our `_updateSquareStatuses` method takes a square's indices as arguments (again), and it begins by looking up the square's frequency and distance data, as seen in this code:

```
def _updateSquareStatus(self, i, j):

    freq = self._squareFreqs[j, i]
    dist = self._squareDists[j, i]
```

We are also interested in the frequency and distance data of a neighboring square that may potentially contain a shadow. As discussed earlier, the user may configure a shadow's direction. The following code shows how we can select a neighbor based on the shadow's direction:

```
if self._shadowDirection == DIRECTION_UP:
    if j > 0:
        neighborFreq = self._squareFreqs[j - 1, i]
        neighborDist = self._squareDists[j - 1, i]
    else:
        neighborFreq = None
        neighborDist = None
elif self._shadowDirection == DIRECTION_LEFT:
    if i > 0:
        neighborFreq = self._squareFreqs[j, i - 1]
        neighborDist = self._squareDists[j, i - 1]
    else:
        neighborFreq = None
        neighborDist = None
elif self._shadowDirection == DIRECTION_DOWN:
```

```
            if j < self._patternSize[1]:
                neighborFreq = self._squareFreqs[j + 1, i]
                neighborDist = self._squareDists[j + 1, i]
            else:
                neighborFreq = None
                neighborDist = None
        elif self._shadowDirection == DIRECTION_RIGHT:
            if i < self._patternSize[0]:
                neighborFreq = self._squareFreqs[j, i + 1]
                neighborDist = self._squareDists[j, i + 1]
            else:
                neighborFreq = None
                neighborDist = None
    else:
        neighborFreq = None
        neighborDist = None
```

We expect a king's shadow to be a small region (low frequency) that contrasts strongly (high frequency) with the background of a light square. Thus, we will test whether the frequency is below a certain threshold and that the distance is above another threshold, as seen in the following code:

```
castsShadow = \
        neighborFreq is not None and \
        neighborFreq < self.emptyFreqThreshold and \
        neighborDist is not None and \
        neighborDist > self.shadowDistThreshold
```

Remember that the user may configure the thresholds in order to manually adapt our approach to different lighting conditions and color schemes.

 Note that the squares on one edge of the board will not have any neighbors in the shadow's direction, so we just assume that there is no shadow there. We could improve on our approach by analyzing the border areas just past the board's edge.

At this point, we have an idea of whether the neighbor might be a shadow or not, but we still need to consider the current square. We expect a playing piece to be a large object (high frequency), and in the absence of such an object, the square must be empty. This logic is reflected in the following code, which relies on a frequency threshold:

```
if freq < self.emptyFreqThreshold:
    squareStatus = SQUARE_STATUS_EMPTY
else:
```

A playing piece may be either dark or light, and either a pawn or a king. We expect a light playing piece to contrast strongly (high distance) with the background of a dark square, while a dark playing piece will have weaker contrast. Thus, another distance threshold is tested. Moreover, we expect a king to have a long shadow that extends into a neighboring square, while a pawn should have a shorter shadow. The following code reflects these criteria:

```
if dist < self.playerDistThreshold:
    if castsShadow:
        squareStatus = SQUARE_STATUS_KING_PLAYER_1
    else:
        squareStatus = SQUARE_STATUS_PAWN_PLAYER_1
else:
    if castsShadow:
        squareStatus = SQUARE_STATUS_KING_PLAYER_2
    else:
        squareStatus = SQUARE_STATUS_PAWN_PLAYER_2
```

At this point, we have a classification result. We will store it so that other methods (and other modules, via a property getter) may access it:

```
self._squareStatuses[j, i] = squareStatus
```

Next, we will provide a convenient way to visualize the classifications of all the squares.

Drawing text

As the last step of updating the image of the board, we will draw text atop each nonempty square to show the numeric code of the classification result. OpenCV provides a function called `cv2.putText(img, text, org, fontFace, fontScale, color, thickness, lineType)` for drawing text at the position specified by the `org` (origin) argument. The origin refers to the top-left corner of the text. However, we want the text to be centered in the square. To find the text's origin relative to the square's center, we need to know the size of the text in pixels. Fortunately, OpenCV provides another function, `cv2.getTextSize(text, fontFace, fontScale, thickness)`, for this purpose. The following code uses these two functions to place the text in the center of a given square:

```
def _drawSquareStatus(self, i, j):

    x0 = i * self._squareWidth
    y0 = j * self._squareWidth

    squareStatus = self._squareStatuses[j, i]
```

```
if squareStatus > 0:
    text = str(squareStatus)
    textSize, textBaseline = cv2.getTextSize(
            text, cv2.FONT_HERSHEY_PLAIN, 1.0, 1)
    xCenter = x0 + self._squareWidth // 2
    yCenter = y0 + self._squareWidth // 2
    textCenter = (xCenter - textSize[0] // 2,
                  yCenter + textBaseline)
    cv2.putText(self._board, text, textCenter,
            cv2.FONT_HERSHEY_PLAIN, 1.0,
            (0, 255, 0), 1, cv2.LINE_AA)
```

Note that we use the `cv2.FONT_HERSHEY_PLAIN` and `cv2.LINE_AA` constants to select the Hershey Plain font and anti-aliasing.

This completes the functionality of the `CheckersModel` class. Next, we write a utility function to convert an OpenCV image for use with wxPython. After this, we will implement the GUI application. It configures an instance of `CheckersModel` and displays the resulting images of the scene and board.

Converting OpenCV images for wxPython

As we have seen earlier, OpenCV treats images as NumPy arrays—typically, 3D arrays in BGR format or 2D arrays in grayscale format. Conversely, wxPython has its own classes for representing images, typically in RGB format (the reverse of BGR). These classes include `wx.Image` (an editable image), `wx.Bitmap` (a displayable image), and `wx.StaticBitmap` (a GUI element that displays a `Bitmap`).

Our `wxUtils` module will provide a function that converts a NumPy array from either BGR or grayscale to an RGB `Bitmap`, ready for display in a wxPython GUI. This functionality depends on OpenCV and wxPython, as reflected in the following `import` statements:

```
from CVBackwardCompat import cv2
import wx
```

Conveniently, wxPython provides a factory function called `wx.BitmapFromBuffer(width, height, dataBuffer)`, which returns a new `Bitmap`. This function can accept a NumPy array in RGB format as the `dataBuffer` argument. However, a bug causes `BitmapFromBuffer` to fail on the first-generation Raspberry Pi, a popular **single-board computer (SBC)**. As a workaround, we can use a pair of functions: `wx.ImageFromBuffer(width, height, dataBuffer)` and `wx.BitmapFromImage(image)`. The latter is less efficient, so we should preferably use it only on hardware that is affected by the bug.

To check whether we are running on the first-generation Pi, we can inspect the name of the system's CPU, as seen in the following code:

```
# Try to determine whether we are on Raspberry Pi.
IS_RASPBERRY_PI = False
try:
    with open('/proc/cpuinfo') as f:
        for line in f:
            line = line.strip()
            if line.startswith('Hardware') and \
                    line.endswith('BCM2708'):
                IS_RASPBERRY_PI = True
                break
except:
    pass
```

Next, let's look at our conversion function's implementation for the first-generation Pi. First, we check the dimensionality of the NumPy array, then make an informed guess about its format (BGR or grayscale), and finally convert it to an RGB array using an OpenCV function called cv2.cvtColor(src, code). The code argument specifies the source and destination formats, such as cv2.COLOR_BGR2RGB. After all of this, we use ImageFromBuffer and BitmapFromImage to convert the RGB array to an Image and the Image to a Bitmap:

```
if IS_RASPBERRY_PI:
    def wxBitmapFromCvImage(image):
        if len(image.shape) < 3:
            image = cv2.cvtColor(image, cv2.COLOR_GRAY2RGB)
        else:
            image = cv2.cvtColor(image, cv2.COLOR_BGR2RGB)
        h, w = image.shape[:2]
        wxImage = wx.ImageFromBuffer(w, h, image)
        bitmap = wx.BitmapFromImage(wxImage)
        return bitmap
```

The implementation for other kinds of hardware is similar, except that we convert the RGB array directly to a Bitmap using BitmapFromBuffer:

```
else:
    def wxBitmapFromCvImage(image):
        if len(image.shape) < 3:
            image = cv2.cvtColor(image, cv2.COLOR_GRAY2RGB)
```

```
else:
    image = cv2.cvtColor(image, cv2.COLOR_BGR2RGB)
h, w = image.shape[:2]
# The following conversion fails on Raspberry Pi.
bitmap = wx.BitmapFromBuffer(w, h, image)
return bitmap
```

We will use this function in our GUI application, coming up next.

Building the GUI application

The `Checkers` module will contain all of the code required for the GUI application. This module depends on wxPython as well as Python's standard `threading` module to allow us to put all of the intensive computer vision work onto a background thread. Moreover, we will rely on our `CheckersModel` module for the capturing and analysis of images, and our WxUtils module for its image conversion utility function. Here are the relevant `import` statements:

```
import threading
import wx

import CheckersModel
import WxUtils
```

Our application class, `Checkers`, is a subclass of `wx.Frame`, which represents a normal window (not a dialog). We initialize it with an instance of `CheckersModel`, and a window title (**Checkers** by default). Here are the declarations of the class and the `__init__` method:

```
class Checkers(wx.Frame):

    def __init__(self, checkersModel, title='Checkers'):
```

We will also store `CheckersModel` in a member variable, like this:

```
        self._checkersModel = checkersModel
```

The implementation of the initializer continues in the following subsections. We will see how the application lays out the GUI, handles events, and interacts with `CheckersModel`.

Creating a window and binding events

We will create a window by initializing the `wx.Frame` superclass. Rather than use the default window style, we will specify a custom style that does not allow the window to be resized. We will also specify the window's title and a gray background color in this code:

```
style = wx.CLOSE_BOX | wx.MINIMIZE_BOX | wx.CAPTION | \
        wx.SYSTEM_MENU | wx.CLIP_CHILDREN
wx.Frame.__init__(self, None, title=title, style=style)
self.SetBackgroundColour(wx.Colour(232, 232, 232))
```

Most wxPython classes inherit a `Bind(event, handler)` method from a high-level class called `EvtHandler`. The method registers a given callback function (`handler`) for a given type of GUI event (`event`). When the object receives an event of the given type, the callback is invoked. For example, let's add the following line of code to ensure that a given method is called when the window is closed:

```
self.Bind(wx.EVT_CLOSE, self._onCloseWindow)
```

The preceding callback is important because our `Checkers` class needs to do some custom cleanup as it closes.

We can also give event bindings an identifier and connect these bindings to keyboard shortcuts via the `wx.AcceleratorTable` class. For example, let's add this code to bind a callback to the *Esc* key:

```
quitCommandID = wx.NewId()
self.Bind(wx.EVT_MENU, self._onQuitCommand,
          id=quitCommandID)
acceleratorTable = wx.AcceleratorTable([
    (wx.ACCEL_NORMAL, wx.WXK_ESCAPE,
     quitCommandID)
])
self.SetAcceleratorTable(acceleratorTable)
```

Later, we will implement the callback such that the *Esc* key makes the window close.

Now that we have a window and a basic grasp of wxPython event binding, let's start putting GUI elements in there!

Creating and laying out images in the GUI

The `wx.StaticBitmap` class is a GUI element that displays a `wx.Bitmap`. Using the following code, let's create a pair of `StaticBitmap` for our images of the scene and the board:

```
self._sceneStaticBitmap = wx.StaticBitmap(self)
self._boardStaticBitmap = wx.StaticBitmap(self)
```

Later, we will implement a helper method to show the `CheckersModel`'s latest images. We will also call this helper now to initialize the `Bitmaps` of `StaticBitmap`:

```
self._showImages()
```

To define the layouts of the `StaticBitmaps` and other wxPython widgets, we must add them to a kind of collection called `wx.Sizer`. It has several direct and indirect subclasses, such as `wx.BoxSizer` (a simple horizontal or vertical layout) and `wx.GridSizer`. For this project, we will use `wx.BoxSizer` only. The following code puts our two `StaticBitmaps` in a horizontal layout, with the scene image first (leftmost) and the board image second:

```
videosSizer = wx.BoxSizer(wx.HORIZONTAL)
videosSizer.Add(self._sceneStaticBitmap)
videosSizer.Add(self._boardStaticBitmap)
```

The rest of the GUI will consist of buttons, a radio box, and sliders, all for the purpose of enabling the user to configure the `CheckersModel`.

Creating and laying out controls

By design, several properties of our `CheckersModel` class must be configured interactively. A person must adjust these parameters while viewing the results of board detection and square classification. Adjustments should be necessary only after the board is initially detected and after any major changes in the lighting.

Remember that the board detector does not limit its search to any range of rotations, and it may choose a rotation in any quadrant. The user may wish to change the rotation to match his or her subjective idea of which way the board is facing. Using the following code, we will create a button labeled **Rotate board CCW**, and we will bind it to a callback that will be responsible for adjusting the rotation by increments of 90 degrees counterclockwise:

```
rotateBoardButton = wx.Button(
        self, label='Rotate board CCW')
rotateBoardButton.Bind(
        wx.EVT_BUTTON,
        self._onRotateBoardClicked)
```

Also remember that the detector may arbitrarily flip the board, since it makes no assumption about whether or not the camera is mirrored. Let's create and bind the **Flip board X** and **Flip board Y** buttons to give the user additional control over the perspective:

```
flipBoardXButton = wx.Button(
        self, label='Flip board X')
flipBoardXButton.Bind(
        wx.EVT_BUTTON,
        self._onFlipBoardXClicked)
flipBoardYButton = wx.Button(
        self, label='Flip board Y')
flipBoardYButton.Bind(
        wx.EVT_BUTTON,
        self._onFlipBoardYClicked)
```

As the square classifier relies on the shadows' direction to determine where the tall king pieces lie, we enable the user to specify the shadows' direction using a **radio box** (a set of radio buttons). The box is labeled **Shadow direction** and the options are **up**, **left**, **down**, and **right**, as specified in the following code:

```
shadowDirectionRadioBox = wx.RadioBox(
        self, label='Shadow direction',
        choices=['up', 'left', 'down', 'right'])
shadowDirectionRadioBox.Bind(
        wx.EVT_RADIOBOX,
        self._onShadowDirectionSelected)
```

Note that the radio buttons in the box are collectively bound to one callback, which is invoked whenever any button is pressed.

Last among the controls, we will provide sliders to configure the classifier's threshold values. These define its expectations about the color contrast in different kinds of squares. The code shown here calls a helper method to make and bind three sliders, labeled **Empty threshold**, **Player threshold**, and **Shadow threshold**:

```
emptyFreqThresholdSlider = self._createLabeledSlider(
        'Empty threshold',
        self._checkersModel.emptyFreqThreshold * 100,
        self._onEmptyFreqThresholdSelected)
playerDistThresholdSlider = self._createLabeledSlider(
        'Player threshold',
        self._checkersModel.playerDistThreshold * 100,
        self._onPlayerDistThresholdSelected)
shadowDistThresholdSlider = self._createLabeledSlider(
```

```
        'Shadow threshold',
        self._checkersModel.shadowDistThreshold * 100,
        self._onShadowDistThresholdSelected)
```

Elsewhere in the `Checkers` class, we implement the following method to help create sliders:

```
    def _createLabeledSlider(self, label, initialValue,
callback):
        slider = wx.Slider(self, size=(180, 20))
        slider.SetValue(initialValue)
        slider.Bind(wx.EVT_SLIDER, callback)
        staticText = wx.StaticText(self, label=label)
        sizer = wx.BoxSizer(wx.VERTICAL)
        sizer.Add(slider, 0, wx.ALIGN_CENTER_
HORIZONTAL)
        sizer.Add(staticText, 0, wx.ALIGN_CENTER_
HORIZONTAL)
        return sizer
```

All our controls will share certain layout properties. They will be centered vertically in their `sizer` and will have 8 pixels of padding on their right-hand side (to separate each control from its neighbor). Let's declare these properties once, like this:

```
controlsStyle = wx.ALIGN_CENTER_VERTICAL | wx.RIGHT
controlsBorder = 8
```

Using these properties, let's add all the controls to a horizontal `sizer`, as seen in the following code:

```
controlsSizer = wx.BoxSizer(wx.HORIZONTAL)
controlsSizer.Add(rotateBoardButton, 0,
                controlsStyle, controlsBorder)
controlsSizer.Add(flipBoardXButton, 0,
                controlsStyle, controlsBorder)
controlsSizer.Add(flipBoardYButton, 0,
                controlsStyle, controlsBorder)
controlsSizer.Add(shadowDirectionRadioBox, 0,
                controlsStyle, controlsBorder)
controlsSizer.Add(emptyFreqThresholdSlider, 0,
                controlsStyle, controlsBorder)
controlsSizer.Add(playerDistThresholdSlider, 0,
                controlsStyle, controlsBorder)
controlsSizer.Add(shadowDistThresholdSlider, 0,
                controlsStyle, controlsBorder)
```

Now we have all our controls in a row!

Nesting layouts and setting the root layout

Sizers can be nested. Let's create a vertical `sizer` and add our two previous `sizers` to it so that our images will appear first (topmost) and our controls second:

```
rootSizer = wx.BoxSizer(wx.VERTICAL)
rootSizer.Add(videosSizer)
rootSizer.Add(controlsSizer, 0, wx.EXPAND | wx.ALL,
              border=controlsBorder)
```

The window should adopt a `sizer` as the root of the layout and should resize itself to fit this layout. The next line of code does this:

```
self.SetSizerAndFit(rootSizer)
```

Now, we have a GUI with a layout and some event bindings, but how do we start running updates to the checkers analyzer?

Starting a background thread

The `CheckersModel` class encapsulates all of the heavy processing in this project, particularly the capture and analysis of images. If we ran its `update()` method on the main thread (which wxPython uses for GUI events), the GUI would become unresponsive, because `update()` would hog the processor all the time. Thus, we must create a background thread that `update()` may safely monopolize. The following code uses Python's standard `threading.Thread` class to run a given function on a new thread:

```
self._captureThread = threading.Thread(
    target=self._runCaptureLoop)
self._running = True
self._captureThread.start()
```

Note that we initialized a member variable, `_running`, before we started the thread. Later, in the implementation of the thread's function, we will use the `_running` variable to control the termination of a loop.

A little later, we will see the implementation of the `_runCaptureLoop()` method, which we have assigned to run on the background thread. First, let's look at the implementations of the callback methods that we have bound to various GUI events.

Closing a window and stopping a background thread

When the window closes, we need to ensure that the background thread terminates normally, meaning that the thread's function must return. The `threading.Thread` class has a method called `join()` that blocks the caller's thread until the callee thread returns. Thus, it allows us to wait for another thread's completion. As we will see later, our background thread continues until `_running` is `False`, so we must set this before calling `join()`. Finally, we must clean up the `wx.Frame` object by calling its `Destroy()` method. Here is the code for the relevant callback:

```
def _onCloseWindow(self, event):
    self._running = False
    self._captureThread.join()
    self.Destroy()
```

 All event callbacks in wxPython require an `event` argument. Depending on the type of event, the `event` argument may have properties that give details about the user's input or other circumstances.

The window will close (and the preceding callback will be called) when the user clicks on the standard close button (**X**), or when we call the `wx.Frame` objects `Close()` method. Remember that we want the window to close when the user presses the *Esc* key. Thus, the *Esc* key is mapped to the following callback:

```
def _onQuitCommand(self, event):
    self.Close()
```

The rest of our callbacks relate to controls that represent the analyzer's configuration.

Configuring the analyzer based on user input

Remember that the `CheckersModel` class has a `boardRotation` property. This is an integer in the range of 0 to 3, representing counterclockwise rotation in 90-degree increments. The property's setter uses a modulus operator to ensure that a value of 4 circles back to 0, and so on. Thus, when the user clicks on the GUI's **Rotate board CCW** button, we can simply increment `boardRotation`, like this:

```
def _onRotateBoardClicked(self, event):
    self._checkersModel.boardRotation += 1
```

Similarly, when the user clicks on the **Flip board X** or **Flip board Y** button, we can negate the value of the `flipBoardX` or `flipBoardY` property (remember that these properties are booleans). Here are the relevant callbacks:

```
def _onFlipBoardXClicked(self, event):
    self._checkersModel.flipBoardX = \
        not self._checkersModel.flipBoardX
def _onFlipBoardYClicked(self, event):
    self._checkersModel.flipBoardY = \
        not self._checkersModel.flipBoardY
```

Like the `boardRotation` property, the `shadowDirection` property is an integer that represents a counterclockwise rotation in 90-degree increments. The options in the **Shadow direction** control box are arranged in the same order (**up**, **right**, **down**, and **left**). Conveniently, wxPython gives the selected option's index to the callback in `event.Selection`. We can assign this index to the `shadowDirection` property, as seen in the following code:

```
def _onShadowDirectionSelected(self, event):
    self._checkersModel.shadowDirection = event.Selection
```

The threshold properties (`emptyFreqThreshold`, `playerDistThreshold`, and `shadowDistThreshold`) are floating-point numbers in the range of `0.0` to `1.0`. By default, wxPython's sliders interpret the user's input as an integer in the range of 0 to 100. Thus, when the user moves a slider, we change the corresponding threshold to one-hundredth of the slider's value, as seen in these callbacks:

```
def _onEmptyFreqThresholdSelected(self, event):
    self._checkersModel.emptyFreqThreshold = \
        event.Selection * 0.01
def _onPlayerDistThresholdSelected(self, event):
    self._checkersModel.playerDistThreshold = \
        event.Selection * 0.01
def _onShadowDistThresholdSelected(self, event):
    self._checkersModel.shadowDistThreshold = \
        event.Selection * 0.01
```

As the user changes the properties, the effect on the classification should be visible in real time, or with only a momentary lag. Let's consider how to update and display the results.

Updating and showing images

On the background thread, the application will continually ask its `CheckersModel` instance to update the images and the analysis. Whenever an update succeeds, the application must alter its GUI to show the new images. This GUI event must be processed on the main (GUI) thread; otherwise, the application will crash, because two threads cannot access the GUI objects at once. Conveniently, wxPython provides a function called `wx.CallAfter(callableObj)` to call a target function (or some other callable object) on the main thread. The following code implements our background thread's loop, which terminates when `_running` is `False`:

```
def _runCaptureLoop(self):
    while self._running:
        if self._checkersModel.update():
            wx.CallAfter(self._showImages)
```

On the main thread, we get the `CheckersModel` images of the unprocessed scene and the processed board, convert them to wxPython's `Bitmap` format using our utility function, and display them in the application's `StaticBitmap`. These two methods carry out this work:

```
def _showImages(self):
    self._showImage(
        self._checkersModel.scene, self._sceneStaticBitmap,
        self._checkersModel.sceneSize)
    self._showImage(
        self._checkersModel.board, self._boardStaticBitmap,
        self._checkersModel.boardSize)
def _showImage(self, image, staticBitmap, size):
    if image is None:
        # Provide a black bitmap.
        bitmap = wx.EmptyBitmap(size[0], size[1])
    else:
        # Convert the image to bitmap format.
        bitmap = WxUtils.wxBitmapFromCvImage(image)
    # Show the bitmap.
    staticBitmap.SetBitmap(bitmap)
```

This is the end of the `Checkers` class, but we still need one more function in the `Checkers` module.

Running the application

Let's write a `main()` function to launch an instance of the `Checkers` application class. This function must also create the application's instance of `CheckersModel`. We will allow the user to specify the camera index as a command-line argument. For example, if the user runs the following command, `CheckersModel` will use a camera index of 1:

```
$ python Checkers.py 1
```

Here is the `main()` function's implementation:

```
def main():
    import sys
    if len(sys.argv) < 2:
        cameraDeviceID = 0
    else:
        cameraDeviceID = int(sys.argv[1])
    checkersModel = CheckersModel.CheckersModel(
            cameraDeviceID=cameraDeviceID)
    app = wx.App()
    checkers = Checkers(checkersModel)
    checkers.Show()
    app.MainLoop()

if __name__ == '__main__':
    main()
```

That's all for the code! Let's grab a webcam and a checkers set!

Troubleshooting the project in real-world conditions

Although this project should work with many checkers sets, camera perspectives, and lighting setups, it still requires the user to set the stage carefully, in accordance with the following guidelines:

1. Ensure that the webcam and the board are stationary. The webcam should be on a tripod or some other mount. The board should also be secured in place, or it should be sufficiently heavy so that it does not move when the players touch it.

2. Leave the board empty until the application detects it and displays the bird's-eye view. If there are playing pieces on the board, they will probably interfere with the initial detection.

3. For best results, use a black-and-white checkerboard. Other color schemes (such as dark wood and light wood) *may* work.

4. For best results, use a board with a light border around the playing area.

5. Also, for best results, use a board with a matte finish or no finish. Reflections on a glossy board will probably interfere with the analysis of the dominant colors in some squares.

6. Put the playing pieces on the dark squares.

7. Use playing pieces that are not of the same color as the dark squares. For example, on a black and white board, use red and white (or red and gray) pieces.

8. Use playing pieces that are sufficiently tall. A king (a pair of stacked pieces) must cast a shadow on an adjacent square.

9. Ensure that the scene has bright light coming predominantly from one direction, such as daylight from a window. Also ensure that the board is aligned such that the light is approximately parallel to the x or y gridlines. Thus, a kings' shadow will fall on an adjacent light square.

Experiment with various real-world conditions and various settings in the application to see what works and what fails. Every computer vision system has limits. Like a person, it does not see everything clearly, and it does not understand all that it sees. As part of our testing process, we should always strive to find the system's limits. This will drive us to adopt or invent more robust techniques for our future work.

Further reading on OpenCV

Our checkers application gives a glimpse of the world of computer vision. Yet, there is much more to see! For Python programmers, the following books from Packt Publishing reveal a broad range of OpenCV's functionality, with impressive applications:

- *Learning OpenCV 3 Computer Vision with Python* (October 2015), by *Joe Minichino* and *Joseph Howse*: This is a grand tour of OpenCV's Python interface and the underlying theories in computer vision, machine learning, and artificial intelligence. With a gentle learning curve, it is suitable for either beginners or those who want to round out their knowledge of the library and its uses.

- *Raspberry Pi Computer Vision Programming* (May 2015), by *Ashwin Pajankar*: This beginner-friendly book emphasizes techniques that are practical for low-cost, low-powered platforms such as the Raspberry Pi single-board computers.

- *OpenCV for Secret Agents* (January, 2015), by *Joseph Howse*: This is a collection of creative, adventurous projects for intermediate to advanced developers who may be new to computer vision. If you want to perform a biometric recognition of a cat or see people's heartbeats through a motion-amplifying webcam, then this is the (only) book for you!

Besides these options, Packt Publishing offers more than a dozen other books on OpenCV and computer vision for C++, Java, Python, iOS, and Android developers. We hope to meet you again in an exploration of this exciting and burgeoning topic!

Summary

While analyzing a game of checkers, we encountered several fundamental aspects of computer vision in the following tasks:

- Capturing images from a camera
- Performing computations on color and grayscale data
- Detecting and recognizing a set of features (the corners of the board's squares)
- Tracking movements of the features
- Simulating a different perspective (a bird's-eye view of the board)
- Classifying the regions of the image (the contents of the board's squares)

We also set up and used OpenCV and other libraries. Having built a complete application using these libraries, you are in a better position to understand the potential of computer vision and plan further studies and projects in this field.

This chapter also concludes our journey together in *Python Game Programming by Example*. We built modern versions of classic video games as well as an analyzer for a classic board game. Along the way, you gained practical experience in many of the major game engines, graphics APIs, GUI frameworks, and scientific libraries for Python. These skills are transferable to other languages and libraries, and will serve as your foundation again and again as you build your own games and other pieces of visual software!

Go create some more great projects, share the fun, and stay in touch with us (Alejandro Rodas de Paz at `alexrdp90@gmail.com` and Joseph Howse at `http://nummist.com/`)!

Index

A

AARectShape class 33
Actor 36
add_ball method 13
add_brick method 13
add(obj) method 32
analyzer
  access, providing to classification
       results 171, 172
  access, providing to images 171, 172
  access, providing to parameters for
       user configuration 172, 173
  bird's -eye view, creating 182-184
  board's corners, detecting 179-182
  board's motion, tracking 179-182
  building 170, 171
  contents of square, classifying 186, 187
  dominant colors, analyzing in
       square 185, 186
  entire game model, initializing 174-176
  entire game model, updating 176, 177
  image, capturing 178
  image, converting 178
  text, drawing 188, 189
Apple Python 163
Arbiter 140
arrival behavior 86, 87
augmented reality 155

B

ball
  collisions 15-19
  movement 15-18
Ball class 9, 10

basic game objects

adding, to game layer 100-102
board game
  features 154, 155
Breakout game
  overview 2, 3
  playing 22
Breakout items
  adding 12-15
  game object instantiation 13
  key input binding 13
Brick class 11, 12

C

cameras
  configuring 166, 167
canvas widget
  canvas.bind() method 7
  canvas.coords() method 7
  canvas.create_text() method 7
  canvas.delete() method 7
  canvas.find_overlapping() method 7
  canvas.find_withtag() method 7
  canvas.itemconfig () method 7
  canvas.move() method 7
  canvas.unbind ()method 7
  canvas.winfo_width() method 7
  references, URL 8
Canvas widget 6, 7
check_collisions method 20
Checkers application
  planning 156-159
Chimpunk2D
  URL 135
CircleShape class 33

enemies 70, 71
slots 69, 70
turret 69, 70

U

update_lives_text method 14
update method 16

V

values, wander behavior
angle_change 90
circle_distance 90
circle_radius 90
wander_angle 90

W

wander behavior
about 89-91
values 90
Windows
setting up 160, 161
URL 160
wxPython
about 154
OpenCV images, converting 189-191
URL 154, 161

X

Xcode Command Line Tools 162

Thank you for buying
Python Game Programming By Example

About Packt Publishing

Packt, pronounced 'packed', published its first book, *Mastering phpMyAdmin for Effective MySQL Management*, in April 2004, and subsequently continued to specialize in publishing highly focused books on specific technologies and solutions.

Our books and publications share the experiences of your fellow IT professionals in adapting and customizing today's systems, applications, and frameworks. Our solution-based books give you the knowledge and power to customize the software and technologies you're using to get the job done. Packt books are more specific and less general than the IT books you have seen in the past. Our unique business model allows us to bring you more focused information, giving you more of what you need to know, and less of what you don't.

Packt is a modern yet unique publishing company that focuses on producing quality, cutting-edge books for communities of developers, administrators, and newbies alike. For more information, please visit our website at www.packtpub.com.

About Packt Open Source

In 2010, Packt launched two new brands, Packt Open Source and Packt Enterprise, in order to continue its focus on specialization. This book is part of the Packt Open Source brand, home to books published on software built around open source licenses, and offering information to anybody from advanced developers to budding web designers. The Open Source brand also runs Packt's Open Source Royalty Scheme, by which Packt gives a royalty to each open source project about whose software a book is sold.

Writing for Packt

We welcome all inquiries from people who are interested in authoring. Book proposals should be sent to author@packtpub.com. If your book idea is still at an early stage and you would like to discuss it first before writing a formal book proposal, then please contact us; one of our commissioning editors will get in touch with you.

We're not just looking for published authors; if you have strong technical skills but no writing experience, our experienced editors can help you develop a writing career, or simply get some additional reward for your expertise.

Expert Python Programming

ISBN: 978-1-84719-494-7   Paperback: 372 pages

Best practices for designing, coding, and distributing your Python software

1. Learn Python development best practices from an expert, with detailed coverage of naming and coding conventions.

2. Apply object-oriented principles, design patterns, and advanced syntax tricks.

3. Manage your code with distributed version control.

4. Profile and optimize your code.

Mobile Game Design Essentials

ISBN: 978-1-84969-298-4   Paperback: 358 pages

A useful and detailed resource for designing games for mobile devices

1. Packed with the best practices in game development, and the methodologies and tricks to create fun, polished games.

2. Detailed descriptions of software and methodologies to create graphics and audio for video games.

3. References to the most popular programming and scripting languages and development kits.

Please check **www.PacktPub.com** for information on our titles

Python High Performance Programming

ISBN: 978-1-78328-845-8   Paperback: 108 pages

Boost the performance of your Python programs using advanced techniques

1. Identify the bottlenecks in your applications and solve them using the best profiling techniques.

2. Write efficient numerical code in NumPy and Cython.

3. Adapt your programs to run on multiple processors with parallel programming.

Learning IPython for Interactive Computing and Data Visualization

ISBN: 978-1-78216-993-2   Paperback: 138 pages

Learn IPython for interactive Python programming, high-performance numerical computing, and data visualization

1. A practical step-by-step tutorial which will help you to replace the Python console with the powerful IPython command-line interface.

2. Use the IPython notebook to modernize the way you interact with Python.

3. Perform highly efficient computations with NumPy and Pandas.

4. Optimize your code using parallel computing and Cython.

Please check **www.PacktPub.com** for information on our titles

52922538R00130

Made in the USA
San Bernardino, CA
01 September 2017